REMEMBER THAT?

A YEAR-BY-YEAR CHRONICLE OF FUN FACTS, HEADLINES, & YOUR MEMORIES

BY ALLISON DOLAN AND THE EDITORS OF
FAMILY TREE MAGAZINE

FAMILY TREE BOOKS

Cincinnati, Ohio
shopfamilytree.com

For more genealogy resources, visit **<shopfamilytree.com>**.

15 14 13 12 11   5 4 3 2 1

ISBN 13: 978-1-4403-1688-3

Distributed in Canada
by Fraser Direct
100 Armstrong Ave.
Georgetown, Ontario, Canada L7G 5S4
Tel: (905) 877-4411

Distributed in the U.K and Europe by
F&W Media International, LTD
Brunel House, Forde Close, Newton Abbot,
TQ12 4PU, UK
Tel: (+44) 1626 323200,
Fax: (+44) 1626 323319
E-mail: enquiries@fwmedia.com

Distributed in Australia
by Capricorn Link
P.O. Box 704, Windsor, NSW 2756 Australia
Tel: (02) 4577-3555

Publisher/Editorial Director: Allison Dolan
Editors: Dana McCullough, Jacqueline Musser, Jamie Royce
Designer: Christy Miller
Production Coordinator: Mark Griffin

How to use this book

Remember That? puts a new twist on the classic almanac. Inside you'll find fascinating facts for the years 1930-2010, from headlines to government affairs to technology and discoveries to new products to sports and pop culture. You'll also have an opportunity to add facts, dates, and favorite memories from your own family.

Every year contains a Family Milestones page that lets you record the major events including births, graduations, marriages, and deaths. You can also write down where your family lived, the jobs you worked or the year in school you completed, the cars you drove, the trips you took, the technology you bought, and the songs and movies you loved. You can use the "People We Loved" prompt to record the names of friends, crushes, sweethearts, partners, and spouses. You can rank your top three memories for each year and there's even room to write a paragraph or two about your favorite memory if you wish.

Involve the entire family—grandparents, parents, and children—for hours of interesting conversations. Working together will help you remember all those long-ago years. Flip through old photos, letters, journals, and yearbooks to revive even more memories.

Use the blank facts pages for the years 2011–2015 to record history as it happens. You can use top-stories-of-the-year news features to help you fill in the blanks. And don't forget to continue to add to your Family Milestones pages as you reach them.

1930

TOP NEWS STORIES: 4.5 million unemployed. More than 1,300 banks fail. U.S. suffers worst-ever drought, causing hardship in farming communities and leading to "Dust Bowl" years. **GOVERNMENT:** President Herbert Hoover signs the 1930 Smoot-Hawley Tariff bill, which raises duties on imports. Congress establishes the Veterans Administration. **CENSUS RESULTS:** U.S. Population 122,775,046 **MEMORABLE SONGS:** "Get Happy" by Harold Arlen • "Happy Feet" by Jack Yellen • "I Got Rhythm" by George and Ira Gershwin • "Little White Lies" by Walter Donaldson • "Lucky Seven" by Howard Dietz • "Mysterious Mose" by Walter Doyle • "Puttin' on the Ritz" by Harry Richman • "Three Little Words" by Duke Ellington and Bing Crosby • "The White Dove" by Clifford Grey

MEMORABLE MOVIES: *All Quiet on the Western Front* • *Hell's Angels* • *The Big House* • *The Divorcee* • *The Blue Angel*

SPORTS: NFL Championship: Green Bay Packers • World Series: Philadelphia Athletics • ABL Championship: Cleveland Rosenblums • Stanley Cup: Montreal Canadiens • Wimbledon: Bill Tilden and Helen Wills Moody • U.S. Open: John Doeg and Betty Nuthall Shoemaker **CELEBRITY BIRTHS:** Buzz Aldrin • Neil Armstrong • Warren Buffet • Ray Charles • Sean Connery • Clint Eastwood • Gene Hackman • Steve McQueen • Princess Margaret • Sandra Day O'Connor • Harold Pinter • J.P. Richardson (aka "The Big Bopper") **TRANSPORTATION:** United Airlines hires the first airline stewardesses. 1930 Cadillac "V-16" is the first production car to offer a 16-cylinder engine. **TECHNOLOGY:** Jet Engine is patented in the United Kingdom. World's first television drama is broadcast in the United Kingdom.

INVENTIONS: Scotch tape • chocolate chip cookie

NEW PRODUCTS: Commercially sold frozen foods • Twinkies • Snickers **DISCOVERIES:** Clyde Tombaugh discovers Pluto, the ninth planet in our solar system (see 2006). Human egg cell is viewed through a microscope for the first time. **FADS:** Irish Sweepstakes established. Mickey Mouse dolls are a popular toy. **CULTURE:** Chrysler Building in New York is completed. Dutch elm disease breaks out in Ohio. The comic strip "Blondie" by Chic Young debuts in Chicago.

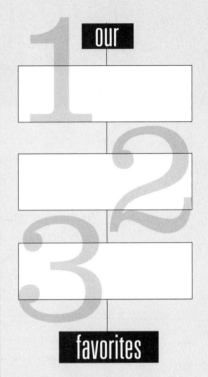

our

1

2

3

favorites

MILK
$0.65/gallon

GAS
$0.25/gallon

NEW HOME
$7,146

AVERAGE INCOME
$1,612/year

FAMILY Milestones

WHERE WE LIVED: ....

....

....

JOBS WE WORKED OR YEAR IN SCHOOL: ....

....

....

CARS WE DROVE: ....

....

PEOPLE WE LOVED: ....

....

SONGS WE LOVED: ....

....

MOVIES WE LOVED: ....

....

TRIPS WE TOOK: ....

....

TECHNOLOGY WE BOUGHT: ....

....

MAJOR MILESTONES: ....

» Births: ....

....

» Graduations: ....

....

» Marriages: ....

....

» Deaths: ....

....

favorite memory...

....

....

....

....

....

1931

TOP NEWS STORIES: 2,300 banks fail; panic spreads. Unemployment tops 8 million. Al Capone is jailed for tax evasion. Chicago Tunnel Explosion and Fire.

GOVERNMENT: Nevada legalizes gambling. President Hoover's Wichersham Committee reports that Prohibition is not working.

MEMORABLE SONGS: "Dream a Little Dream of Me" by Wayne King • "Goodnight, Sweetheart" by Guy Lombardo • "Just a Gigolo" by Ted Lewis • "Minnie the Moocher" by Cab Calloway • "Mood Indigo" by Duke Ellington • "Smile Darn Ya Smile" by Ben Seliv • "Stardust" by Ishham Jones **MEMORABLE MOVIES:** *The Champ* • *Cimmaron* • *City Lights* • *Dracula* • *Dr. Jekyll and Mr. Hyde* • *Frankenstein* • *The Guardsman* • *The Maltese Falcon* • *Mata Hari* • *The Painted Desert* • *The Public Enemy* • *Skippy* **SPORTS:** NFL Championship: Green Bay Packers • World Series: St. Louis Cardinals • ABL Championship: Brooklyn Visitations • Stanley Cup: Montreal Canadiens • Wimbledon: Sidney Wood and Cilly Aussem • U.S. Open: Ellsworth Vines and Helen Wills Moody **CELEBRITY BIRTHS:** Anne Bancroft • James Dean • Angie Dickinson • Olympia Dukakis • Robert Duvall • James Earl Jones • Larry Hagman • Tab Hunter • Rita Moreno • Rupert Murdoch • Leonard Nimoy • Regis Philbin • Dan Rather • Della Reese • William Shatner • Willie Shoemaker • Desmond Tutu • Boris Yeltsin **TRANSPORTATION:** Ford ends production of the Ford Model A and prepares for the new Ford V8. George Washington Bridge opens connecting New York and New Jersey. **TECHNOLOGY:** Vannevar Bush finishes developing the Bush Differential Analyzer, the first analog computer. **INVENTIONS:** Electric razor • nylon • aerosol can • fiberglass • neoprene rubber • radio antenna **NEW PRODUCTS:** Alka-Seltzer • Clairol hair dye **DISCOVERIES:** Wiley Post and Harold Gatty fly *Winnie Mae* around the world in less than nine days. J.G. Lansky discovers radio waves from outer space. **FADS:** Fortean Society is founded to ridicule science. **CULTURE:** Empire State Building is completed, and becomes the tallest building in the world. "The Star Spangled Banner" becomes the U.S. national anthem. Work begins on the Boulder Dam (later named Hoover Dam). Popular radio shows were *The Easy Aces* and *Little Orphan Annie*.

our

favorites

MILK
$0.50/gallon

GAS
$0.10/gallon

NEW HOME
$6,796

AVERAGE INCOME
$1,527/year

FAMILY Milestones

WHERE WE LIVED: ....

....

....

JOBS WE WORKED OR YEAR IN SCHOOL: ....

....

....

CARS WE DROVE: ....

....

PEOPLE WE LOVED: ....

....

SONGS WE LOVED: ....

....

MOVIES WE LOVED: ....

....

TRIPS WE TOOK: ....

....

TECHNOLOGY WE BOUGHT: ....

....

MAJOR MILESTONES:

» Births: ....

....

» Graduations: ....

....

» Marriages: ....

....

» Deaths: ....

....

1932

TOP NEWS STORIES: Lindbergh baby is kidnapped. Police in Dearborn, Michigan, fire into a crowd of demonstrators outside Ford Motor Co. plant. Between 13 and 17 million are unemployed. **GOVERNMENT:** Franklin D. Roosevelt and John N. Garner elected president and vice president. Congress releases 85 million bushels of wheat to feed starving Americans. The first federal gasoline tax, part of the Revenue Act of 1932 taxes, applies a 1 cent per gallon tax on imported gasoline and fuel oil. **MEMORABLE SONGS:** "All Of Me" by Louis Armstrong • "April in Paris" by E.G. Harburg • "Eadie Was a Lady" by B.G. DeSylva • "Eres Tu" by Miguel Sandoval • "Louisiana Hayride" by Howard Dietz • "Mimi" by Lorenz Hart • "So Do I" by B.G. DeSylva • "Three's a Crowd" by Al Dubin • "Willow Weep for Me" by Irving Berlin **MEMORABLE MOVIES:** *Bird of Paradise* • *A Farewell to Arms* • *Freaks* • *The Mummy* • *One Hour With You* • *Prestige* • *Scarface* • *The Sign of the Cross* • *Tarzan, The Ape Man* • *Trouble in Paradise* • *Vampyr* **SPORTS:** NFL Championship: Chicago Bears • World Series: New York Yankees • ABL Championship: Brooklyn Visitations • Stanley Cup: Toronto Maple Leafs • Wimbledon: Ellsworth Vines • Indianapolis 500: Fred Frame • U.S. Open: Ellsworth Vines and Helen Jacobs • Winter Olympic Games: Lake Placid, NY • Summer Olympic Games: Los Angeles **CELEBRITY BIRTHS:** Ellen Burstyn • Johnny Cash • Petula Clark • Patsy Cline • Jenny Craig • Ted Kennedy • Loretta Lynn • Peter O'Toole • Debbie Reynolds • Charles Rich • Little Richard • Donald Rumsfeld • Omar Sharif • Elizabeth Taylor • John Updike • Robert Vaughn • John Williams

---

TRANSPORTATION: Route 66 opens between Chicago and Los Angeles. Boeing Model 247, the first modern airliner, is patented. Amelia Earhart becomes the first woman to make a solo air crossing of the Atlantic Ocean.

TECHNOLOGY: BBC television beings first regular broadcasts. Ernest Orlando Lawrence builds world's first cyclotron. **INVENTIONS:** Polaroids • parking meter **NEW PRODUCTS:** Zippo lighter • 3 Musketeers bar • Fritos corn chips • Skippy peanut butter • Big Little Books **DISCOVERIES:** Dr. Charles Glen King isolates vitamin C. **FADS:** Betty Boop becomes popular. **CULTURE:** Revlon is founded. Radio City Music Hall opens in New York City. Work begins on the Golden Gate Bridge.

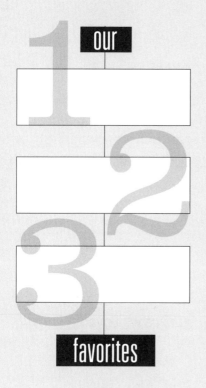

our

1

2

3

favorites

MILK
$0.43/gallon

GAS
$0.18/gallon

NEW HOME
$6,515

AVERAGE INCOME
$1,431/year

FAMILY Milestones

WHERE WE LIVED: ....

....

....

JOBS WE WORKED OR YEAR IN SCHOOL: ....

....

....

CARS WE DROVE: ....

....

PEOPLE WE LOVED: ....

....

SONGS WE LOVED: ....

....

MOVIES WE LOVED: ....

....

TRIPS WE TOOK: ....

....

TECHNOLOGY WE BOUGHT: ....

....

MAJOR MILESTONES:

» Births: ....

....

» Graduations: ....

....

» Marriages: ....

....

» Deaths: ....

....

favorite memory

....

....

....

....

....

1933

TOP NEWS STORIES: Alcatraz officially becomes a federal prison. Federal Deposit Insurance Corp (FDIC) becomes effective. Strong winds strip the topsoil from the drought-affected farms in Midwest, creating Dust Bowls. **GOVERNMENT:** Franklin D. Roosevelt sworn in as U.S. president. The 21st Amendment repeals Prohibition. President Roosevelt gives his first "fireside chat" in a radio broadcast, and he launches the New Deal. **MEMORABLE SONGS:** "Dinner at Eight" by Dorothy Fields • "Easter Parade" by Irving Berlin • "It Isn't Fair" by Richard Himber • "I Wanna Be Loved" by Billy Rose • "On the Trail" by Ferdie Grofe • "Shadow Waltz" by Al Dubin • "Temptation" by Arthur Freed • "Tony's Wife" by Harold Adamson **MEMORABLE MOVIES:** *42nd Street* • *Alice in Wonderland* • *Cavalcade* • *Duck Soup* • *Going Hollywood* • *The Invisible Man* • *King Kong* • *Little Women* • *Morning Glory* **SPORTS:** NFL Championship: Chicago Bears • World Series: New York Giants • Stanley Cup: New York Rangers • Wimbledon: Jack Crawford and Susan Schenfield • U.S. Open: Fred Perry and Helen Jacobs • PGA Championship: Gene Sarazen **CELEBRITY BIRTHS:** Carol Burnett • Michael Caine • Joan Collins • Michael Dukakis • Jerry Falwell • Dianne Feinstein • Marty Feldman • Ruth Bader Ginsberg • Quincy Jones • Larry King • Jayne Mansfield • Elizabeth Montgomery • Willie Nelson • Yoko Ono • Roman Polanski • Joan Rivers • Tom Skerritt • Cicely Tyson • Johnny Unitas • Gene Wilder **TRANSPORTATION:** Wiley Post becomes the first man to fly solo around the world. **TECHNOLOGY:** Children in the western world begin receiving diphtheria inoculation. **INVENTIONS:** frequency modulation (FM) **NEW PRODUCTS:** *Esquire* and *Newsweek* magazines **DISCOVERIES:** The Loch Ness Monster is first sighted in modern times. **FADS:** Speakeasies of the Prohibition era become cafés or chic restaurants. The Dy-Dee-Doll drinks water from a bottle and wets its diaper. First drive-in movie theater opens.

CULTURE: Pennsylvania opens the first state-run liquor stores in the United States. Helen Jacobs wears shorts in tennis tournaments. Albert Einstein arrives in the United States. Sally Rand does the fan dance at the Chicago World's Fair. Budweiser Clydesdale horses appear the day after Prohibition ends.

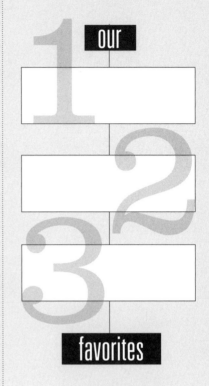

our

1

2

3

favorites

MILK
$0.41/gallon

GAS
$0.18/gallon

NEW HOME
$5,759

AVERAGE INCOME
$1,409/year

FAMILY
Milestones

WHERE WE LIVED: ....

....

....

JOBS WE WORKED OR YEAR IN SCHOOL:

....

....

CARS WE DROVE: ....

....

PEOPLE WE LOVED: ....

....

SONGS WE LOVED: ....

....

MOVIES WE LOVED: ....

....

TRIPS WE TOOK: ....

....

TECHNOLOGY WE BOUGHT: ....

....

MAJOR MILESTONES: ....

» Births: ....

....

» Graduations: ....

....

» Marriages: ....

....

» Deaths: ....

....

favorite memory

....

....

....

....

....

....

19 34

TOP NEWS STORIES: Bruno R. Hauptmann trial begins for kidnap-murder of Lindbergh baby. Bonnie Parker and Clyde Barrow are killed. Dionne sisters are first successful birth of quintuplets. **GOVERNMENT:** Securities and Exchange Commission and Federal Communications Commission are established. Indian Reorganization Act reverses the allotment policy. National Labor Relations Board is created. American Liberty League is founded to oppose New Deal economic measures. **MEMORABLE SONGS:** "Fair and Warmer" by Al Dubin • "Fun to be Fooled" by Ira Gershwin • "Lost in a Fog" by Dorothy Fields • "On the Good Ship Lollipop" by Shirley Temple • "One Night of Love" by Gus Kahn • "Solitude" by Duke Ellington • "There Goes My Heart" by Abner Silver • "Winter Wonderland" by Richard Himber • "You're the Top" by Cole Porter **MEMORABLE MOVIES:** *Babes in Toyland* • *Cleopatra* • *Death Takes a Holiday* • *The Count of Monte Cristo* • *It Happened One Night* • *Little Miss Marker* • *The Merry Widow* • *The Painted Veil* • *The Scarlet Pimpernel* • *Treasure Island* **SPORTS:** NFL Championship: New York Giants • World Series: St. Louis Cardinals • Stanley Cup: Chicago Blackhawks • World Cup: Italy • Wimbledon: Fred Perry and Dorothy Round • U.S. Open: Fred Perry and Helen Jacobs • PGA Championship: Paul Runyan **CELEBRITY BIRTHS:** Hank Aaron • Alan Arkin • Giorgio Armani • Peter Arnett • Tom Baker • Brigitte Bardot • Pat Boone • Judi Dench • Barbara Eden • Brian Epstein • Yuri Gagarin • Florence Henderson • Barry Humphries • Roy Kinnear • Sophia Loren • Garry Marshall • Charles Manson • Shirley MacLaine • Rue McClanahan • Bill Moyers • Ralph Nader • Sydney Pollack **TRANSPORTATION:** Helen Richey becomes first woman to pilot an airmail transport. **TECHNOLOGY:** *Flying Scotsman* is first steam locomotive to be officially recorded at 100 miles per hour. **INVENTIONS:** Metal beverage can **NEW PRODUCTS:** Hammond Organ • Ritz Crackers **DISCOVERIES:** Henrik Dam discovers vitamin K.

FADS: Hot toys were Radio Flyer Streak-O-Lite and Parker Brothers' Sorry!

CULTURE: Shirley Temple signs a contract with Twentieth Century Fox. Donald Duck debuts in "The Wise Little Hen." First laundromat opens. Muzak Corporation is founded. "Okies," not all of them from Oklahoma, migrate west to escape Dust Bowl. Great Smoky Mountains National Park is created. Cartoon strips "Lil'l Abner" and "Flash Gordon" debut.

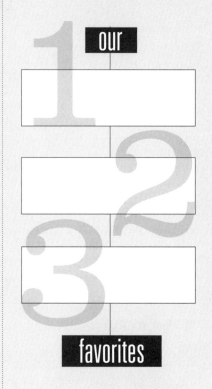

our

1

2

3

favorites

MILK
$0.45/gallon

GAS
$0.19/gallon

NEW HOME
$5,972

AVERAGE INCOME
$1,506/year

FAMILY Milestones

WHERE WE LIVED: ....

....

....

JOBS WE WORKED OR YEAR IN SCHOOL: ....

....

....

CARS WE DROVE: ....

....

PEOPLE WE LOVED: ....

....

SONGS WE LOVED: ....

....

MOVIES WE LOVED: ....

....

TRIPS WE TOOK: ....

....

TECHNOLOGY WE BOUGHT: ....

....

MAJOR MILESTONES:

» Births: ....

....

» Graduations: ....

....

» Marriages: ....

....

» Deaths: ....

....

favorite memory

....

....

....

....

....

1935

TOP NEWS STORIES: Great Labor Day Category 5 Hurricane with winds approaching 185 mph strikes Florida Keys. Works Progress Administration established to create millions of jobs. Feds kill Fred and "Ma" Barker outside of Ocklawaha, Florida **GOVERNMENT:** Second phase of New Deal, calling for social security, better housing, equitable taxation, and farm assistance, begins. Wagner Act forces employers to accept collective bargaining. Rural Electrification Act and Soil Conservation Act are signed into law. **MEMORABLE SONGS:** "Lights Out" by Billy Hill • "Love Me Forever" by Gus Kahn • "Lullaby of Broadway" by Al Dubin • "The Piccolino" by Irving Berlin • "Red Sails in the Sunset" by Guy Lombardo • "This Time It's Love" by Sam Lewis • "Why Shouldn't I?" by Cole Porter • "You're an Angel" by Jimmy McHugh **MEMORABLE MOVIES:** *Anna Karenina* • *Bride of Frankenstein* • *Captain Blood* • *The Informer* • *The Miracle Rider* • *Mutiny on the Bounty* • *Scrooge* • *A Tale of Two Cities* • *Top Hat* **SPORTS:** NFL Championship: Detroit Lions • World Series: Detroit Tigers • ABL Championship: Brooklyn Visitations • Stanley Cup: Montreal Marrons • Wimbledon: Fred Perry and Helen Wills Moody • U.S. Open: Wilmer Allison and Helen Jacobs • PGA Championship: Johnny Revolta • Heisman Trophy: Jay Berwanger

CELEBRITY BIRTHS: Woody Allen • Julie Andrews • Sonny Bono • Peter Boyle • Dalai Lama • Jerry Lee Lewis • Dudley Moore • Luciano Pavarotti • Gary Player • Elvis Presley • Donald Sutherland • Gene Vincent

TRANSPORTATION: *The China Clipper* makes the first Pacific Airmail delivery. Toyota Cars are launched in Japan. United Auto Workers is founded. **TECHNOLOGY:** GE starts selling the first fluorescent tube for light. **INVENTIONS:** Richter scale • polyethylene (the most widely used plastic) **NEW PRODUCTS:** Monopoly board game • canned beer (Krueger Beer is the first) **DISCOVERIES:** Uranium-235 **FADS:** Benny Goodman introduces "big band" jazz music. **CULTURE:** Penguin produces the first paperback books. Alcoholics Anonymous is founded in New York City. The Gallup Poll is introduced. Mae West earns second largest salary in the United States.

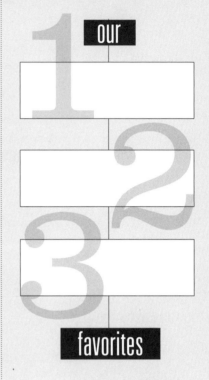

our 1 2 3 favorites

MILK
$0.47/gallon

GAS
$0.19/gallon

NEW HOME
$6,296

AVERAGE INCOME
$1,594/year

FAMILY Milestones

WHERE WE LIVED: ....

....

....

JOBS WE WORKED OR YEAR IN SCHOOL: ....

....

....

CARS WE DROVE: ....

....

PEOPLE WE LOVED: ....

....

SONGS WE LOVED: ....

....

MOVIES WE LOVED: ....

....

TRIPS WE TOOK: ....

....

TECHNOLOGY WE BOUGHT: ....

....

MAJOR MILESTONES: ....

» Births: ....

....

» Graduations: ....

....

» Marriages: ....

....

» Deaths: ....

....

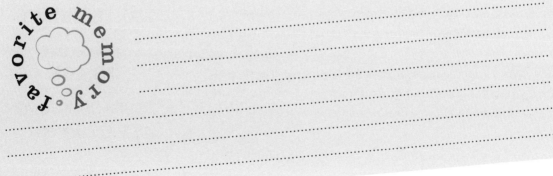

19 36

TOP NEWS STORIES: Sit-down strikes spread across the nation. GM accepts the United Auto Workers (UAW) as the bargaining agent for striking workers.

GOVERNMENT: Voters re-elect Franklin D. Roosevelt as president. **MEMORABLE SONGS:** "Alone" by Tommy Dorsey • "Did I Remember" by Shep Fields • "A Fine Romance" by Fred Astaire • "Goody, Goody" by Benny Goodman • "Is It True What They Say about Dixie?" by Jimmy Dorsey • "It's a Sin to Tell a Lie" by Fats Waller • "The Music Goes Round and Round" by Tommy Dorsey • "Pennies from Heaven" by Bing Crosby • "The Way You Look Tonight" by Fred Astaire **MEMORABLE MOVIES:** *The Charge of the Light Brigade* • *Dracula's Daughter* • *The Great Ziegfeld* • *Follow the Fleet* • *Fury* • *Modern Times* • *Mr. Deeds Goes to Town* • *Poor Little Rich Girl* • *Three Smart Girls* **SPORTS:** NFL Championship: Green Bay Packers • World Series: New York Yankees • Stanley Cup: Detroit Red Wings • U.S. Open: Fred Perry and Alice Marble • Wimbledon: Fred Perry and Helen Jacobs • PGA Championship: Denny Shute • Summer Olympics: Jesse Owens win four gold medals **CELEBRITY BIRTHS:** Alan Alda • Ursula Andress • Robert "Bo" Belinsky • Glen Campbell • David Carradine • Wilt Chamberlain • Charlie Daniels • Bobby Darin • Don Drysdale • Jim Henson • Buddy Holly • Dennis Hopper • Kris Kristoferson • Michael Landon • John McCain • Mary Tyler Moore • Roy Orbison • Robert Redford • Burt Reynolds • Yves Saint Laurent **TRANSPORTATION:** Douglas Aircraft introduces the DC-3. First successful helicopter flight is made. *Queen Mary* luxury liner makes her maiden voyage across the Atlantic. The LZ 129 *Hindenburg*, a German zeppelin, makes its first flight. **TECHNOLOGY:** Alan Turing submits his famous paper "On Computable Numbers" for publication. **INVENTIONS:** artificial heart **NEW PRODUCTS:** 35mm Kodachrome film • Waring blender • *Life* magazine **DISCOVERIES:** Vitamin E is isolated. Catalytic cracking (a process that increased gasoline production) lowers gas production. **FADS:** Jive talk includes the words *alligator, canary, hepcat, in the groove*, and *long hair*. **CULTURE:** *The Joy of Cooking* is published. Boulder Dam (later named Hoover Dam) is completed. Margaret Mitchell's *Gone With the Wind* is published. *Billboard Magazine* publishes the first pop music chart.

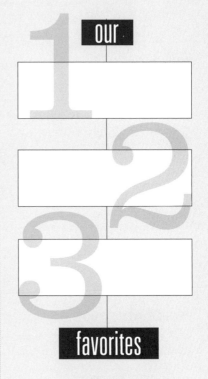

our

1

2

3

favorites

$

MILK
$0.48/gallon

GAS
$0.19/gallon

NEW HOME
$6,145

AVERAGE INCOME
$1,672/year

FAMILY
Milestones

WHERE WE LIVED: ....

....

....

JOBS WE WORKED OR YEAR IN SCHOOL: ....

....

....

CARS WE DROVE: ....

....

PEOPLE WE LOVED: ....

....

SONGS WE LOVED: ....

....

MOVIES WE LOVED: ....

....

TRIPS WE TOOK: ....

....

TECHNOLOGY WE BOUGHT: ....

....

MAJOR MILESTONES: ....

» Births: ....

....

» Graduations: ....

....

» Marriages: ....

....

» Deaths: ....

....

favorite memory...

....

....

....

....

....

....

19 37

TOP NEWS STORIES: Ohio River flood leaves 500,000 homeless. Amelia Earhart disappears while on a flight around the world. **GOVERNMENT:** Franklin D. Roosevelt tries to pack the Supreme Court. The Marijuana Traffic Act outlaws possession and sale of marijuana. Steel companies accept United Steel Workers Union as their union bargaining agent. **MEMORABLE SONGS:** "That Old Feeling" by Shep Fields • "Once In Awhile" by Tommy Dorsey • "It Looks Like Rain in Cherry Blossom Lane" by Guy Lombardo • "September In the Rain" by Guy Lombardo • "The Dipsy Doodle" by Tommy Dorsey • "Sweet Leilani" by Bing Crosby • "The Moon Got In My Eyes" by Bing Crosby • "Boo Hoo" by Guy Lombardo • "Goodnight, My Love" by Benny Goodman • "Whispers In the Dark" by Bob Crosby **MEMORABLE MOVIES:** *The Awful Truth* • *Captains Courageous* • *Conquest* • *A Day at the Races* • *Shall We Dance* • *Snow White and the Seven Dwarfs* • *A Star is Born* • *Topper Way Out West* **SPORTS:** NFL Championships: Washington Redskins • World Series: New York Yankees • Stanley Cup: Detroit Red Wings • World Figure Skating Championship: Megan Taylor (Great Britain) and Felix Kaspar (Austria) • U.S. Open: Don Budge and Anita Lizana • Wimbledon: Don Budge and Dorothy Round • PGA Championship: Denny Shute **CELEBRITY BIRTHS:** Madeline Albright • Shirely Bassey • Warren Beatty • Bobby Charlton • Jackie Collins • Peter Cook • Bill Cosby • Bobby Driscoll • Don Everly • Jane Fonda • Morgan Freeman • Merle Haggard • Dustin Hoffman • Anthony Hopkins • Jack Nicholson • Roger Penske • Colin Powell • Vanessa Redgrave • Kenny Rogers • Bob Schieffer • Ridley Scott • Loretta Swit • Marlo Thomas **TRANSPORTATION:** The airship *Hindenburg* explodes upon her arrival in Lakehurst, New Jersey. The Golden Gate Bridge is dedicated. GM introduces an automatic transmission for cars. **TECHNOLOGY:** A prototype "antihistamine" is produced to treat allergies.

INVENTIONS: Nylon • photocopying

NEW PRODUCTS: Spam • shopping carts • Sellotape (cellophane tape) • *Look* and *Newsweek* magazines **DISCOVERIES:** Hans Krebs postulates the "cycle" of oxidative phoshorylation, the basic process of cellular metabolism. **FADS:** Fashionable men sport Panama hats. **CULTURE:** Howard Johnson restaurants open for business. John Steinbeck's *Of Mice and Men* and J. R. R. Tolkien's *The Hobbit* are published. Walt Disney's first animated feature-length film, *Snow White and the Seven Dwarfs*, hits theaters.

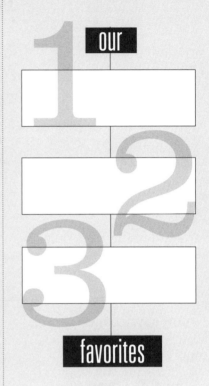

our
1
2
3
favorites

MILK
$0.50/gallon

GAS
$0.20/gallon

NEW HOME
$6,622

AVERAGE INCOME
$1,789/year

FAMILY
Milestones

WHERE WE LIVED: ....

....

....

JOBS WE WORKED OR YEAR IN SCHOOL:

....

....

CARS WE DROVE: ....

....

PEOPLE WE LOVED: ....

....

SONGS WE LOVED: ....

....

MOVIES WE LOVED: ....

....

TRIPS WE TOOK: ....

....

TECHNOLOGY WE BOUGHT: ....

....

MAJOR MILESTONES: ....

» Births: ....

....

» Graduations: ....

....

» Marriages: ....

....

» Deaths: ....

....

favorite memory

....

....

....

....

....

....

19**38**

TOP NEWS STORIES: A one-time science fiction special, *The War of the Worlds*, causes widespread hysteria. Unemployment reaches 19 percent. Unexpected hurricane wreaks havoc on Long Island, New York, and in New England. **GOVERNMENT:** Congress passes a Flood Control Act authorizing public works projects. Fair Labor Standards Law sets minimum wages at $0.25 per hour. House Committee on Un-American Activities is established. **MEMORABLE SONGS:** "A-Tisket, A-Tasket" by Ella Fitzgerald with Chick Webb • "Begin the Beguine" by June Knight • "Cry, Baby, Cry" by Larry Clinton • "Jeepers Creepers" by Louis Armstrong • "I've Got a Pocketful of Dreams" by Bing Crosby • "Music, Maestro, Please" by Tommy Dorsey • "My Reverie" by Larry Clinton • "Thanks for the Memory" by Shep Fields • "Whistle While You Work" by Adriana Caselotti • "You Must Have Been a Beautiful Baby" by Dick Powell **MEMORABLE MOVIES:** *The Adventures of Robin Hood* • *Boys Town* • *Bringing Up Baby* • *A Christmas Carol* • *Holiday* • *Jezebel* • *Marie Antoinette* • *Love Finds Andy Hardy* • *Test Pilot* • *Too Hot to Handle* **SPORTS:** NFL Championship: New York Giants • World Series: New York Yankees • NBL Championship: Akron Goodyear Wingfoots • Stanley Cup: Chicago Blackhawks • World Cup: Italy • World Figure Skating Championship: Megan Taylor (Great Britain) and Felix Kaspar (Austria) • U.S. Open: Alice Marble and Don Budge • Wimbledon: Helen Moody and Don Budge • PGA Championship: Paul Runyan **CELEBRITY BIRTHS:** Kofi Annan • Wolfman Jack • Peter Jennings • Evel Knievel • Christopher Lloyd • Bernie Madoff • Don "Dandy Don" Meredith • Janet Reno • Oscar Robertson • Ted Turner • Jon Voight • Natalie Wood

---

TECHNOLOGY: The self-propelled combine is introduced.

TRANSPORTATION: Volkswagen introduces the Beetle. **INVENTIONS:** Ballpoint pen • Teflon • fiberglass • xerography **NEW PRODUCTS:** Nylon toothbrushes **DISCOVERIES:** Shock therapy is used to treat mental illness. **FADS:** Brenda Frazier sets the fashion trend with a strapless evening gown. **CULTURE:** March of Dimes is established to fight polio. City National Bank of South Bend, Indiana, introduces drive-through banking. Thornton Wilder writes the play *Our Town*. *The Green Hornet* is a popular radio show. Superman character debuts in *Action Comics*. The Glenn Miller Orchestra forms.

our

favorites

$

MILK
$0.50/gallon

GAS
$0.20/gallon

NEW HOME
$6,420

AVERAGE INCOME
$1,808/year

MINIMUM WAGE
$0.25/hour

FAMILY Milestones

WHERE WE LIVED: ....

....

....

JOBS WE WORKED OR YEAR IN SCHOOL:

....

....

CARS WE DROVE: ....

....

PEOPLE WE LOVED: ....

....

SONGS WE LOVED: ....

....

MOVIES WE LOVED: ....

....

TRIPS WE TOOK: ....

....

TECHNOLOGY WE BOUGHT: ....

....

MAJOR MILESTONES: ....

» Births: ....

....

» Graduations: ....

....

» Marriages: ....

....

» Deaths: ....

....

19**39**

TOP NEWS STORIES: Jewish refugees aboard the SS *St. Louis* are denied entry into the United States. **GOVERNMENT:** Congress passes the Hatch Act. Albert Einstein sends a letter to Roosevelt explaining the potential of an atomic bomb. U.S. Department of Agriculture starts first food stamp program in Rochester, New York.

MEMORABLE SONGS: "And the Angels Sing" by Benny Goodman • "Beer Barrel Polka" by Will Glahe • "Deep Purple" by Larry Clinton • "God Bless America" by Kate Smith • "Moon Love" by Glenn Miller • "Over the Rainbow" by Glenn Miller (also Judy Garland) • "Scatter-Brain" by Frankie Masters • "South of the Border" by Shep Fields • "Stairway to the Stars" by Glenn Miller • "Wishing (Will Make It So)" by Glenn Miller

---

MEMORABLE MOVIES: *Destry Rides Again* • *Gone With the Wind* • *The Hunchback of Notre Dame* • *The Little Princess* • *Mr. Smith Goes to Washington* • *Stagecoach* • *The Wizard of Oz* (starring Judy Garland) **SPORTS:** NFL Championship: Green Bay Packers • World Series: New York Yankees • NBL Championship: Akron Firestone No-Skids • Stanley Cup: Boston Bruins • World Figure Skating Championship: Megan Taylor (Great Britain) and Graham Sharp (Great Britain) • PGA Championship: Henry Picard • U.S. Open: Alice Marble and Bobby Riggs • Wimbledon: Alice Marble and Bobby Riggs **CELEBRITY BIRTHS:** John Amos • Frankie Avalon • Francis Ford Coppola • Mike Ditka • Marvin Gaye • George Hamilton • Carolina Hererra • Paul Hogan • Ralph Lauren • Cynthia Lennon • Ali MacGraw • Lee Majors • Ian McKellen • Maury Povich • Harry Reid • Neil Sedaka • Phil Spector • Dusty Springfield • Lily Tomlin • Tina Turner **TRANSPORTATION:** Pan Am introduces transatlantic air travel. **TECHNOLOGY:** Hewlett-Packard is established. **INVENTIONS:** First electronic digital computer **NEW PRODUCTS:** Precooked frozen foods • nylon stockings **DISCOVERIES:** The Uranium atom is split. **FADS:** Bare midriffs are popular in the summer. Goldfish swallowing on college campuses is popular. **CULTURE:** Batman debuts in *Detective Comics*. Bugs Bunny cartoons debut.

our

1

2

3

favorites

$

MILK
$0.49/gallon

GAS
$0.19/gallon

NEW HOME
$6,416

AVERAGE INCOME
$1,837/year

MINIMUM WAGE
$0.30/hour

FAMILY Milestones

WHERE WE LIVED: ....

....

....

JOBS WE WORKED OR YEAR IN SCHOOL: ....

....

....

CARS WE DROVE: ....

....

PEOPLE WE LOVED: ....

....

SONGS WE LOVED: ....

....

MOVIES WE LOVED: ....

....

TRIPS WE TOOK: ....

....

TECHNOLOGY WE BOUGHT: ....

....

MAJOR MILESTONES:

» Births: ....

....

» Graduations: ....

....

» Marriages: ....

....

» Deaths: ....

....

favorite memory...

....

....

....

....

....

19 40

TOP NEWS STORY: The first peacetime draft goes into effect. **GOVERNMENT:** Franklin D. Roosevelt and Henry Wallace are elected president and vice president. Alien Registration Act passes. **CENSUS RESULTS:** U.S. population is 131,669,275. In the previous decade 528,431 immigrants entered the U.S. **MEMORABLE SONGS:** "Blueberry Hill" by Sammy Kaye Orchestra • "Frenesi" by Artie Shaw • "I'll Never Smile Again" by Tommy Dorsey with Frank Sinatra • "In the Mood" by Glenn Miller • "Only Forever" by Bing Crosby • "Tuxedo Junction" by Glenn Miller • "When You Wish Upon a Star" by Glenn Miller • "You Are My Sunshine" by Jimmie Davis **MEMORABLE MOVIES:** *Fantasia* • *The Grapes of Wrath* • *Pinocchio* • *Road to Singapore*

SPORTS: NFL Championship Game: Chicago Bears • World Series: Cincinnati Reds • Stanley Cup: New York Rangers • NBL Championship: Akron Firestone Non-Skids • PGA Championship: Byron Nelson • U.S. Open: Alice Marble and Don McNeill

---

CELEBRITY BIRTHS: Tom Brokaw • James Brolin • Peter Fonda • Bobby Knight • Ted Koppel • Bruce Lee • John Lennon • Jack Nicklaus • Chuck Norris • Al Pacino • Pele • Nancy Pelosi • Smokey Robinson • Martin Sheen • Ringo Starr • Alex Trebek • Raquel Welch **TRANSPORTATION:** The first U.S. superhighway, the Pennsylvania Turnpike, opens. **TECHNOLOGY:** Edward R. Murrow begins broadcasting from London.

INVENTIONS: Electron microscope

NEW PRODUCTS: M&Ms (developed for GIs) **DISCOVERIES:** Wilhelm Reich builds his orgone energy accumulator to concentrate a special energy to cure human ills. **FADS:** The Lindy Hop dance is popular. Zoot suits are fashionable. **CULTURE:** Charles R. Drew opens the first blood bank, but isn't allowed to donate because of segregation laws. The 40-hour work week goes into effect. Popular radio shows include *Gangbusters*, *Fibber McGee and Molly*, and *The Jack Benny Show*.

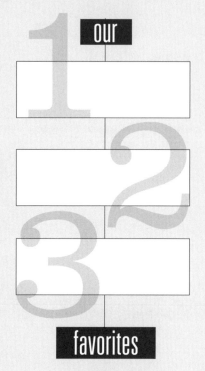

our

1
2
3

favorites

$

MILK
$0.51/gallon

GAS
$0.18/gallon

NEW HOME
$6,558

AVERAGE INCOME
$1,906/year

MINIMUM WAGE
$0.30/hour

FAMILY
Milestones

WHERE WE LIVED: ....

....

....

JOBS WE WORKED OR YEAR IN SCHOOL: ....

....

....

CARS WE DROVE: ....

....

PEOPLE WE LOVED: ....

....

SONGS WE LOVED: ....

....

MOVIES WE LOVED: ....

....

TRIPS WE TOOK: ....

....

TECHNOLOGY WE BOUGHT: ....

....

MAJOR MILESTONES: ....

» Births: ....

....

» Graduations: ....

....

» Marriages: ....

....

» Deaths: ....

....

favorite memory...

....

....

....

....

....

19 41

TOP NEWS STORIES: Japan attacks Pearl Harbor, Hawaii, drawing America into World War II. Unemployment is 10 percent.

GOVERNMENT: President Roosevelt talks of Four Freedoms in his State of the Union speech. Roosevelt and Winston Churchill agree on Atlantic Charter. Racial discrimination is outlawed in the defense industry. **MEMORABLE SONGS:** "Amapola" by Jimmy Dorsey • "Chattanooga Choo Choo" by Glenn Miller • "Daddy" by Sammy Kaye • "God Bless the Child" by Billie Holiday • "Green Eyes" by Jimmy Dorsey • "I Don't Want to Set the World On Fire" by Hoarce Heidt • "Maria Elena" by Jimmy Dorsey • "There I Go" by Vaughn Monroe • "There'll Be Some Changes Made" by Benny Goodman • "You and I" by Glenn Miller **MEMORABLE MOVIES:** *Buck Privates* • *Citizen Kane* • *Dumbo* • *The Maltese Falcon* • *Sergeant York* • *The Wolf Man* **SPORTS:** NFL Championship: Chicago Bears • World Series: New York Yankees • NBL Championship: Oshkosh All-Stars • Stanley Cup: Boston Bruins • U.S. Open: Sarah Palfrey Cooke and Bobby Riggs • PGA Championship: Vic Ghezzi **CELEBRITY BIRTHS:** Paul Anka • Beau Bridges • Dick Cheney • Neil Diamond • Plácido Domingo • Faye Dunaway • Bob Dylan • Nora Eprhon • Jesse Jackson • Ann Margret • Nick Nolte • Ryan O'Neal • Pete Rose • Paul Simon • Martha Stewart **TRANSPORTATION:** Diesel freight locomotives go into service. **TECHNOLOGY:** Leslie Groves heads the Manhattan Project to develop an atomic bomb. **INVENTIONS:** Electric guitar **NEW PRODUCTS:** Cheerios **DISCOVERIES:** Plutonium is isolated. **FADS:** Short skirts become fashionable as government regulations limit the amount of fabric available. Veronica Lake starts a hairstyle craze with a "peek-a-boo" look.

CULTURE: "Rosie the Riveter" popularizes the American woman's role in defense industries. "Sad Sack" appears in military newspapers. Mount Rushmore National Monument is completed. Greta Garbo retires from public life. Popular radio shows are *The Red Skelton Show* and *The Thin Man.*

$

MILK
$0.34/gallon

GAS
$0.19/gallon

NEW HOME
$6,954

AVERAGE INCOME
$2,059/year

MINIMUM WAGE
$0.30/hour

FAMILY Milestones

WHERE WE LIVED: ....

....

....

JOBS WE WORKED OR YEAR IN SCHOOL: ....

....

....

CARS WE DROVE: ....

....

PEOPLE WE LOVED: ....

....

SONGS WE LOVED: ....

....

MOVIES WE LOVED: ....

....

TRIPS WE TOOK: ....

....

TECHNOLOGY WE BOUGHT: ....

....

MAJOR MILESTONES: ....

» Births: ....

....

» Graduations: ....

....

» Marriages: ....

....

» Deaths: ....

favorite memory

....

....

....

....

....

19**42**

TOP NEWS STORIES: United States defeats Japan in Battles of the Coral Sea and Midway. U.S. troops invade North Africa. U.S. Marines use Navajo Code Talkers in the Pacific theater. Western Allies condemn Nazi death camps. **GOVERNMENT:** Executive order 9066 interns 110,000 Japanese-Americans. The Congress of Racial Equity (CORE) is founded. Minimum draft age is lowered from 21 to 18. **MEMORABLE SONGS:** "(I've Got a Gal in) Kalamazoo" by Glenn Miller • "Jingle, Jangle, Jingle" by Kay Kyser • "Moonlight Cocktail" by Glenn Miller • "Tangerine" by Jimmy Dorsey • "White Christmas" by Bing Crosby

MEMORABLE MOVIES: *Arabian Nights • Casablanca • Bambi • For Me and My Gal • Holiday Inn • Mrs. Miniver • Yankee Doodle Dandy*

SPORTS: NFL Championship: Washington Redskins • World Series: St. Louis Cardinals • NBL Championship: Oshkosh All-Stars • Stanley Cup: Toronto Maple Leafs • U.S. Open: Pauline Betz Addie and Ted Schroeder • PGA Championship: Sam Snead **CELEBRITY BIRTHS:** Isabel Allende • Joe Biden • Dick Butkus • Michael Crichton • Roger Ebert • Linda Evans • Harrison Ford • Jerry Garcia • Stephen Hawking • Isaac Hayes • Jimi Hendrix • John Irving • Carole King • Paul McCartney • Wayne Newton • Marin Scorses • Barbra Streisand • Tammy Wynette **TRANSPORTATION:** Alaska Highway is completed. **TECHNOLOGY:** Radar comes into operational use.

INVENTIONS: Guided missile • nuclear reactor • napalm • magnetic recording tape

NEW PRODUCTS: Duct tape **DISCOVERIES:** The first controlled nuclear chain reaction is achieved at the University of Chicago. **FADS:** People begin hoarding due to rationing of food stuffs and essentials. Polyesters for clothing are introduced. Sales of women's trousers skyrocket. **CULTURE:** U.S. adopts Daylight Savings Time. Victory Gardens are cultivated. Voice of America begins broadcasting. Popular radio shows are *People Are Funny* and *Suspense.* "Chattanooga Choo-Choo" becomes the first gold record.

our
1
2
3
favorites

$

MILK
$0.60/gallon

GAS
$0.20/gallon

NEW HOME
$7,573

AVERAGE INCOME
$2,348/year

MINIMUM WAGE
$0.30/hour

FAMILY
Milestones

WHERE WE LIVED: ....

....

....

JOBS WE WORKED OR YEAR IN SCHOOL: ....

....

....

CARS WE DROVE: ....

....

PEOPLE WE LOVED: ....

....

SONGS WE LOVED: ....

....

MOVIES WE LOVED: ....

....

TRIPS WE TOOK: ....

....

TECHNOLOGY WE BOUGHT: ....

....

MAJOR MILESTONES:

» Births: ....

....

» Graduations: ....

....

» Marriages: ....

....

» Deaths: ....

....

favorite memory

....

....

....

....

....

....

1943

TOP NEWS STORIES: United States' living standard is one-third higher than in 1939. Allies achieve victory in invasions of Sicily and Italy, Battle of the Bismarck Sea and Guadalcanal in the Pacific. **GOVERNMENT:** Congress passes a "pay-as-you-go" Tax Payment Act. The Pentagon is completed. President freezes prices, salaries, and wages to prevent inflation. Chinese Exclusion Acts of 1882 and 1902 are repealed. **MEMORABLE SONGS:** "As Time Goes By" by Rudy Vallee • "I'll Be Home for Christmas" by Bing Crosby • "I've Heard That Song Before" by Harry James • "Paper Doll" by Mills Brothers • "Pistol Packin' Mama" by Al Dexter • "Sunday, Monday or Always" by Bing Crosby • "That Old Black Magic" by Glenn Miller **MEMORABLE MOVIES:** *Batman* • *Coney Island* • *Heaven Can Wait* • *Jitterbugs* • *The Ox-Bow Incident* • *Sahara* • *Shadow of a Doubt* • *Titanic* **SPORTS:** NFL Championship: Chicago Bears • World Series: New York Yankees • NBL Championship: Sheboygan Redskins • Stanley Cup: Detroit Red Wings • U.S. Open: Pauline Betz Addie and Joseph Hunt

---

CELEBRITY BIRTHS: Chevy Chase • Jim Croce • Robert De Niro • John Denver • Charlie Gibson • Newt Gingrich • George Harrison • Mick Jagger • Janis Joplin • Barry Manilow • Penny Marshall • Joe Pesci • Keith Richards • Geraldo Rivera • Christopher Walken • Bob Woodward

---

TRANSPORTATION: Car companies produce bombs and aircraft engines for war effort. **TECHNOLOGY:** Edward Noble founds ABC. **INVENTIONS:** Silly Putty • scuba gear **NEW PRODUCTS:** Milton Bradley's Snakes (Chutes) and Ladders board game **DISCOVERIES:** Selman Wasksman discovers the antibiotic streptomycin. Medical establishment recognizes the Pap test for detecting cervical cancer. **FADS:** Jitterbug is a popular dance. **CULTURE:** Cartoonist Bill Mauldin draws "Willie and Joe" for the Army newspaper *Stars and Stripes*. Americans must "use it up, wear it out, make it do, or do without." Andrew Wyeth paints "The Hunter." Popular radio shows are *Perry Mason* and *Nick Carter, Master Detective*. Rodgers and Hammerstein's *Oklahoma!* initiates new era of the American musical. All-American Girls Professional Baseball is formed.

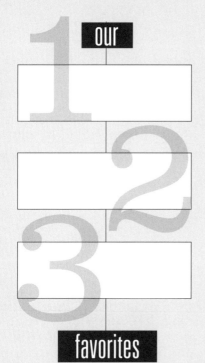

our
1
2
3
favorites

$

MILK
$0.62/gallon

GAS
$0.21/gallon

NEW HOME
$8,011

AVERAGE INCOME
$2,561/year

MINIMUM WAGE
$0.30/hour

FAMILY
Milestones

WHERE WE LIVED: ....

....

....

JOBS WE WORKED OR YEAR IN SCHOOL:

....

....

CARS WE DROVE: ....

....

PEOPLE WE LOVED: ....

....

SONGS WE LOVED: ....

....

MOVIES WE LOVED: ....

....

TRIPS WE TOOK: ....

....

TECHNOLOGY WE BOUGHT: ....

....

MAJOR MILESTONES: ....

» Births: ....

....

» Graduations: ....

....

» Marriages: ....

....

» Deaths: ....

....

19**44**

TOP NEWS STORIES: Battles in Europe include D-Day at Normandy, Anzio Beach in Italy, and the Battle of the Bulge. Soviet forces discover the Majdanek concentration camp.

GOVERNMENT: The Supreme Court rules that Americans cannot be denied the right to vote due to color. FDR elected to fourth term; Harry Truman elected vice president. Congress passes the GI Bill of Rights.

MEMORABLE SONGS: "Don't Fence Me In" by Bing Crosby & The Andrews Sisters • "I'll Be Seeing You" by Bing Crosby • "I Love You" by Bing Crosby • "I'm Making Believe" by Ella Fitzgerald and The Ink Spots • "Mairzy Doats" by Merry Macs • "Swinging On a Star" by Bing Crosby • "You Always Hurt the One You Love" by The Mills Brothers **MEMORABLE MOVIES:** *Arsenic and Old Lace* • *Going My Way* • *Meet Me in St. Louis* • *National Velvet* **SPORTS:** NFL Championship: Green Bay Packers • World Series: St. Louis Cardinals • Stanley Cup: Montreal Canadiens • NBL Championship: Fort Wayne Zollner Pistons • PGA Championship: Bob Hamilton • U.S. Open: Pauline Betz Addie and Frank Parker **CELEBRITY BIRTHS:** Carl Bernstein • Peter Cetera • Stockard Channing • Joe Cocker • Danny DeVito • Michael Douglas • Steve Fossett • Dennis Franz • Rudy Giuliani • Gladys Knight • Patti LaBelle • Brenda Lee • George Lucas • Craig T. Nelson • Tony Orlando • Diana Ross • Jerry Springer • Alice Walker • Barry White

TRANSPORTATION: Boeing's XF8B-1 (Model 400) long-range Navy fighter plane makes its first flight.

TECHNOLOGY: A general-purpose digital computer is built at Harvard. **INVENTIONS:** Assault rifle • sunscreen **NEW PRODUCTS:** Kodacolor film • *Seventeen* magazine **DISCOVERIES:** DDT is used to control body lice. Oswald Avery isolates DNA. **FADS:** Both men's and women's clothing features broad padded shoulders. Besides bobbysocks, teens wear baggy jeans with shirttails hanging out. **CULTURE:** Popular radio shows are *The Adventures of Ozzie and Harriet* and *Roy Rogers*.

our

1

2

3

favorites

$

MILK
$0.62/gallon

GAS
$0.21/gallon

NEW HOME
$8,649

AVERAGE INCOME
$2,675/year

MINIMUM WAGE
$0.30/hour

FAMILY Milestones

WHERE WE LIVED: ....

....

....

JOBS WE WORKED OR YEAR IN SCHOOL: ....

....

....

CARS WE DROVE: ....

....

PEOPLE WE LOVED: ....

....

SONGS WE LOVED: ....

....

MOVIES WE LOVED: ....

....

TRIPS WE TOOK: ....

....

TECHNOLOGY WE BOUGHT: ....

....

MAJOR MILESTONES: ....

» Births: ....

....

» Graduations: ....

....

» Marriages: ....

....

» Deaths: ....

....

19 45

TOP NEWS STORIES: World War II ends when Germany surrenders May 8 and Japan surrenders September 2. United States drops the first atomic bomb, "Little Boy," on Hiroshima. A B-25 bomber crashes into the Empire State Building 78th and 79th floors, killing 13. **GOVERNMENT:** Franklin D. Roosevelt dies; Harry Truman is sworn in as President. **MEMORABLE SONGS:** "My Dreams are Getting Better All the Time" by Les Brown • "On the Atcheson, Topeka, & the Santa Fe" by Johnny Mercer • "Rum & Coca-Cola" by The Andrews Sisters • "Sentimental Journey" by Les Brown and Doris Day • "Till the End of Time" by Perry Como **MEMORABLE MOVIES:** *The Bells of St. Mary's* • *Christmas in Connecticut* • *The Lost Weekend* • *Rhapsody in Blue* • *Spellbound* **SPORTS:** NFL Championship: Cleveland Rams • World Series: Detroit Tigers • NBL Championship: Fort Wayne Zollner Pistons • Stanley Cup: Toronto Maple Leafs • U.S. Open: Sarah Palfrey Cooke and Frank Parker • PGA Championship: Byron Nelson **CELEBRITY BIRTHS:** Jerry Bruckheimer • Eric Clapton • Mia Farrow • Goldie Hawn • Davy Jones • Dean Koontz • John Lithgow • Steve Martin • Don McLean • Bette Midler • Helen Mirren • Anne Murray • Diane Sawyer • Tom Selleck • Carly Simon • Rod Stewart • Henry Winkler **TRANSPORTATION:** Henry Ford appoints his grandson Henry Ford II as president of Ford Motor Company. Lincoln and Mercury merge into a single division.

TECHNOLOGY: Water fluoridation is introduced to prevent cavities. ENIAC computer is completed. Discovery of a moth lodged in a relay of the Harvard Mark II computer leads to the term "computer bug."

INVENTIONS: Microwave oven **NEW PRODUCTS:** Streptomycin • penicillin • aerosol spray cans • ballpoint pens • Tupperware • *Ebony* magazine • Ertl Die Cast Toys **DIS-COVERIES:** American Cyanamid Corporation discovers folic acid.

FADS: Slinky toy becomes popular.

CULTURE: Food rationing ends. FCC sets aside channels for commercial TV. *Meet the Press* is a popular radio show. Rodgers and Hammerstein's *Carousel* musical opens on Broadway.

our 1 2 3 favorites

$

MILK
$0.62/gallon

GAS
$0.21/gallon

NEW HOME
$10,131

AVERAGE INCOME
$2,807/year

MINIMUM WAGE
$0.40/hour

FAMILY Milestones

WHERE WE LIVED: ....

....

....

JOBS WE WORKED OR YEAR IN SCHOOL: ....

....

....

CARS WE DROVE: ....

....

PEOPLE WE LOVED: ....

....

SONGS WE LOVED: ....

....

MOVIES WE LOVED: ....

....

TRIPS WE TOOK: ....

....

TECHNOLOGY WE BOUGHT: ....

....

MAJOR MILESTONES: ....

» Births: ....

....

» Graduations: ....

....

» Marriages: ....

....

» Deaths: ....

....

favorite memory...

....

....

....

....

....

19 46

TOP NEWS STORIES: President Harry S. Truman seizes mines and railroads as millions of workers strike for better pay. Consumers demonstrate against inflation when price and wage controls are lifted. **GOVERNMENT:** Congress establishes the Atomic Energy Commission and Indian Claims Commission. Fulbright scholarship program begins.

MEMORABLE SONGS: "Doin' What Comes Natur'lly" by Ethel Merman • "Five Minutes More" by Frank Sinatra • "(I Love You) For Sentimental Reasons" by Nat King Cole • "Let It Snow! Let It Snow! Let It Snow!" by Vaughn Monroe • "Prisoner of Love" by Perry Como • "Route 66" by Nat King Cole • "To Each His Own" by The Ink Spots • "Zip-a-Dee-Doo-Dah" by James Baskett

MEMORABLE MOVIES: *The Best Years of Our Lives* • *It's a Wonderful Life* • *Night and Day* • *Notorious* • *Stairway to Heaven* • *The Yearling* **SPORTS:** NFL Championship: Chicago Bears • World Series: St. Louis Cardinals • Stanley Cup: Montreal Canadiens • NBL Championship: Rochester Royals • U.S. Open: Pauline Betz Addie and Jack Kramer • PGA Championship: Ben Hogan **CELEBRITY BIRTHS:** André the Giant • Candice Bergen • Jimmy Buffet • George W. Bush • Cher • Bill Clinton • Patty Duke • Sally Field • Danny Glover • Gregory Hines • Tommy Lee Jones • Naomi Judd • Diane Keaton • Susan Lucci • Cheech Marin • Hayley Mills • Liza Minelli • Ed O'Neill • Linda Ronstadt • Dolly Parton • Susan Sarandon • Steve Spielberg • Sylvester Stallone • Suzanne Somers • Donald Trump • Diane von Fürstenberg **TRANSPORTATION:** Boeing signs a contract to design the B-52 bomber **TECHNOLOGY:** Printed circuits are developed. **INVENTIONS:** Carbon-14 dating • freeze-dried foods • waterproof diapers • automatic pinspotter for bowling **NEW PRODUCTS:** Timex watches • Tide laundry detergent **DISCOVERIES:** U.S. Army makes first radar contact with the moon **FADS:** American women sport bikinis. **CULTURE:** Birth rates begin to soar. The first full-time Spanish language station, KCOR-AM, begins airing in San Antonio, Texas. A popular radio program is *Sam Spade*. "Bugsy" Siegel builds the Flamingo Hotel in Las Vegas, Nevada. Dr. Benjamin Spock publishes *The Common Sense Book of Baby and Child Care*. Cannes Film Festival debuts in France.

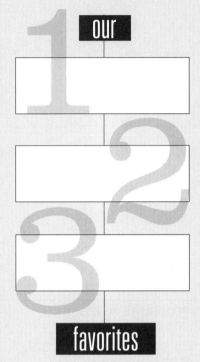

our
1
2
3

favorites

$

MILK
$0.70/gallon

GAS
$0.21/gallon

NEW HOME
$12,638

AVERAGE INCOME
$3,118/year

MINIMUM WAGE
$0.40/hour

FAMILY Milestones

WHERE WE LIVED: ....

....

....

JOBS WE WORKED OR YEAR IN SCHOOL:

....

....

CARS WE DROVE: ....

....

PEOPLE WE LOVED: ....

....

SONGS WE LOVED: ....

....

MOVIES WE LOVED: ....

....

TRIPS WE TOOK: ....

....

TECHNOLOGY WE BOUGHT: ....

....

MAJOR MILESTONES:

» Births: ....

....

» Graduations: ....

....

» Marriages: ....

....

» Deaths: ....

....

favorite memory

19**47**

TOP NEWS STORY: The "Hollywood Ten" are imprisoned for refusing to affirm or deny their membership in the Communist Party. **GOVERNMENT:** U.S. Air Force, National Security Council, and CIA are established. Mexican-American veterans organize the American GI Forum. The Taft-Hartley Act, which forbids closed shops, passes. **MEMORABLE SONGS:** "Ballerina" by Vaughn Monroe • "Chi-Baba, Chi-Baba" by Perry Como • "Heartaches" by Ted Weems • "Near You" by Francis Craig **MEMORABLE MOVIES:** *The Bishop's Wife* • *The Fugitive* • *The Ghost and Mrs. Muir* • *Miracle on 34th Street* **SPORTS:** NFL Championship: Chicago Cardinals • World Series: New York Yankees • Stanley Cup: Toronto Maple Leafs • NBL Championship: Chicago American Geras • World Figure Skating Championship: Barbara Ann Scott (Canada) and Hans Gerschwiler (Switzerland) • Wimbeldon: Margaret Osborne duPont and Jack Kramer • U.S. Open: Louise Brough Clapp and Jack Kramer • PGA Championship: Jim Ferrier **CELEBRITY BIRTHS:** Kareem Abdul-Jabbar • Dave Barry • David Bowie • Tom Clancy • Glenn Close • Stephen Collins • Ted Danson • Paula Dean • Richard Dreyfuss • Farrah Fawcett • Jack Hanna • Don Henley • Elton John • Stephen King • John Larroquette • David Letterman • James Patterson • Iggy Pop • Dan Quayle • Rob Reiner • Hillary Rodham Clinton • Mitt Romney • Nolan Ryan • Carlos Santana • Laura Schlessinger • Arnold Schwarzenegger • O.J. Simpson **TRANSPORTATION:** GM and UAW agree on a cost-of-living raise. The Ford Foundation is established. The first tubeless tires appear. **TECHNOLOGY:** The first microwave relay station begins operation. **INVENTIONS:** Instant photography • transistors • cat litter **NEW PRODUCTS:** Ajax cleanser • Toni hair permanent • Polaroid Land Camera • Reddi-Wip • Almond Joy candy bar

DISCOVERIES: The Bell X-1 rocket plane breaks the sound barrier. Radiocarbon dating is developed.

FADS: American women buy into Christian Dior's lowered skirt lengths, padded bras, unpadded shoulders, and fezzes. The first report of "flying saucers" begins a craze. **CULTURE:** Billy Graham begins preaching at revival meetings. Popular TV shows are *Kraft Television Theatre*, *Howdy Doody*, and *Meet the Press*.

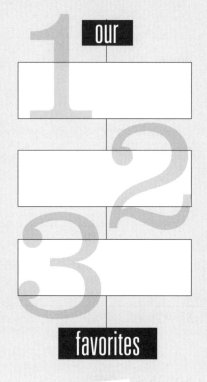

our

1

2

3

favorites

$

MILK
$0.80/gallon

GAS
$0.23/gallon

NEW HOME
$13,000

AVERAGE INCOME
$3,456/year

MINIMUM WAGE
$0.40/hour

FAMILY Milestones

WHERE WE LIVED: ....

....

....

JOBS WE WORKED OR YEAR IN SCHOOL: ....

....

....

CARS WE DROVE: ....

....

PEOPLE WE LOVED: ....

....

SONGS WE LOVED: ....

....

MOVIES WE LOVED: ....

....

TRIPS WE TOOK: ....

....

TECHNOLOGY WE BOUGHT: ....

....

MAJOR MILESTONES: ....

» Births: ....

....

» Graduations: ....

....

» Marriages: ....

....

» Deaths: ....

....

19 48

TOP NEWS STORIES: United States begins the Berlin Airlift after the Soviets seal off the city. A dike along the Columbia River breaks, killing 15 and leaving tens of thousands of people homeless in Vanport, Oregon. **GOVERNMENT:** Harry Truman and Alben Barkley are elected president and vice president. The Selective Service Act becomes law. Truman desegregates the Armed Forces. The Supreme Court declares religious education in public schools unconstitutional. Congress authorizes the Marshall Plan to rebuild Europe. **MEMORABLE SONGS:** "Buttons and Bows" by Dinah Shore • "I'm Looking Over a Four-Leaf Clover" by Art Mooney • "Nature Boy" by Nat King Cole • "Twelfth Street Rag" by Pee Wee Hunt • "Woody Woodpecker" by Kay Kyser **MEMORABLE MOVIES:** *Anna Karenina* • *Easter Parade* • *Key Largo* • *The Pirate* • *Superman* • *The Treasure of the Sierra Madre* **SPORTS:** NFL Championship: Philadelphia Eagles • World Series: Cleveland Indians • Stanley Cup: Toronto Maple Leafs • NBL Championship: Minneapolis Lakers • World Figure Skating Championship: Barbara Ann Scott (Canada) and Dick Button (United States) • Wimbledon: Louise Brough Clapp and Bob Falkenburg • U.S. Open: Pancho Gonzales and Margaret Osborne duDpont • PGA Championship: Ben Hogan **CELEBRITY BIRTHS:** Kathy Bates • Wolf Blitzer • Prince Charles • Alice Cooper • Billy Crystal • Peggy Fleming • Bryant Gumbel • Samuel L. Jackson • Kenny Loggins • Olivia Newton-John • Stevie Nicks • Ted Nugent • Ozzy Osbourne • Rhea Perlman • Bernadette Peters • Raffi • Phylicia Rashad • John Ritter • Cat Stevens • Sally Struthers • Steven Tyler • Steve Winwood **TRANSPORTATION:** Air-conditioning is offered in automobiles. The Land Rover is unveiled at the Amsterdam Motor Show. Ford introduces F-Series truck. **TECHNOLOGY:** Cable TV is introduced. Warner Brothers shows the first color newsreel: The Tournament of Roses Parade and the Rose Bowl. The first monkey astronaut, Albert I, is launched into space. **INVENTIONS:** LP records • Velcro • holography **NEW PRODUCTS:** Dramamine • Dial deodorant soap • Scrabble board game • *U.S. News and World Report* **DISCOVERIES:** Mathematician Norbert Wiener introduces "cybernetics."

FADS: The Pez candy dispenser is introduced.

CULTURE: International Planned Parenthood is founded. The first McDonald's restaurant opens. Popular TV shows include *The Ed Sullivan Show, Fran & Ollie, Hopalong Cassidy, Kukla, The Milton Berle Show,* and *The Perry Como Show.* The comic strip "Pogo" debuts.

our

1

2

3

favorites

$

MILK
$0.86/gallon

GAS
$0.26/gallon

NEW HOME
$13,500

AVERAGE INCOME
$3,671/year

MINIMUM WAGE
$0.40/hour

FAMILY Milestones

WHERE WE LIVED: ....

....

....

JOBS WE WORKED OR YEAR IN SCHOOL:

....

....

CARS WE DROVE: ....

....

PEOPLE WE LOVED: ....

....

SONGS WE LOVED: ....

....

MOVIES WE LOVED: ....

....

TRIPS WE TOOK: ....

....

TECHNOLOGY WE BOUGHT: ....

....

MAJOR MILESTONES: ....

» Births: ....

....

» Graduations: ....

....

» Marriages: ....

....

» Deaths: ....

....

favorite memory

1949

TOP NEWS STORIES: General Motors, Standard Oil of California, Firestone Tire, and other companies are convicted of criminal conspiracy to replace electric transit lines with gasoline or diesel buses. Edith Mae Irby is the first African-American admitted to the University of Arkansas Medical School. Los Angeles receives its first recorded snowfall.

GOVERNMENT: NATO forms. President Harry S. Truman unveils his Fair Deal program. **MEMORABLE SONGS:** "Ghost Riders in the Sky" by Vaughn Monroe • "I Can Dream, Can't I?" by The Andrews Sisters • "Mule Train" by Frankie Laine • "Rudolph, the Red-Nosed Reindeer" by Gene Autry • "Some Enchanted Evening" by Perry Como • "That Lucky Old Sun" by Frankie Laine **MEMORABLE MOVIES:** *Adam's Rib* • *All the King's Men* • *In the Good Old Summertime* • *On the Town* • *The Third Man* • *Twelve O'Clock High* **SPORTS:** NFL Championship: Philadelphia Eagles • World Series: New York Yankees • Stanley Cup: Toronto Maple Leafs • NASCAR Championship: Robert "Red" Byron • NBL Championship: Anderson Packers • Wimbledon: Louise Brough Clapp and Ted Schroeder • U.S. Open: Margaret Osborne duPont and Pancho Gonzales • PGA Championship: Sam Snead • World Figure Skating Championships: Aja Zanova (Czechoslovakia) and Dick Button (United States) **CELEBRITY BIRTHS:** John Belushi • Jeff Bridges • Patrick Duffy • George Foreman • Richard Gere • Billy Joel • Jessica Lange • Annie Leibovitz • Shelley Long • Eddie Money • Wolfgang Puck • Lionel Richie • Gene Simmons • Jane Smiley • Sissy Spacek • Bruce Springsteen • Meryl Streep • Ivana Trump • Sigourney Weaver **TRANSPORTATION:** *Lucky Lady II* completes first circum-global nonstop flight. **TECHNOLOGY:** Soviet Union begins testing atomic weapons. EDSAC, the first stored-program computer, begins operation. **INVENTIONS:** Zamboni ice-resurfacing machine **NEW PRODUCTS:** Cootie game • Candy Land game • LEGO plastic interlocking bricks **DISCOVERIES:** The antibiotics oxytetracycline and neomycin are developed. English astronomer coins the term "Big Bang" during a BBC radio broadcast. **CULTURE:** Miles Davis cuts the first "cool" jazz records. *Dragnet* is a new radio program. Popular TV shows are *The Goldbergs*, *The Life of Riley*, *Red Barber's Corner*, *Crusader Rabbit*, *Captain Video and His Video Rangers*, and *The Lone Ranger*. First Emmy Awards are handed out, with *Pantomime Quiz Time* winning most popular TV program. Rodgers and Hammerstein's *South Pacific* opens on Broadway.

our

1

2

3

favorites

$

MILK
$0.84/gallon

GAS
$0.27/gallon

NEW HOME
$14,300

AVERAGE INCOME
$3,569/year

MINIMUM WAGE
$0.40/hour

FAMILY
Milestones

WHERE WE LIVED: ....

....

....

JOBS WE WORKED OR YEAR IN SCHOOL: ....

....

....

CARS WE DROVE: ....

....

PEOPLE WE LOVED: ....

....

SONGS WE LOVED: ....

....

MOVIES WE LOVED: ....

....

TRIPS WE TOOK: ....

....

TECHNOLOGY WE BOUGHT: ....

....

MAJOR MILESTONES:

» Births: ....

....

» Graduations: ....

....

» Marriages: ....

....

» Deaths: ....

....

....

....

....

....

....

1950

TOP NEWS STORIES: The Korean War begins when North Korea invades South Korea. Puerto Rican nationalists attempt to assassinate President Truman. **GOVERNMENT:** Truman authorizes development of a hydrogen bomb and orders the Army to seize the railroads. Congress establishes the National Science Foundation. **CENSUS RESULTS:** U.S. population is 150,697,361. 1,035,039 immigrants entered the United States in the previous decade. **MEMORABLE SONGS:** "Chattanoogie Shoe Shine Boy" by Red Foley • "Goodnight, Irene" by Red Foley • "I Wanna be Loved" by The Andrews Sisters • "Mona Lisa" by Nat King Cole • "Rag Mop" by The Ames Brothers • "Silver Bells" by Bing Crosby and Carol Richards • "The Tennessee Waltz" by Patti Page **MEMORABLE MOVIES:** *All About Eve* • *Annie Get Your Gun* • *Cinderella* • *Fancy Pants* • *Rio Grande* • *Sunset Boulevard* **SPORTS:** NFL Championship: Cleveland Browns • World Series: New York Yankees • NBA Championship: Minneapolis Lakers • Stanley Cup: Detroit Red Wings • World Cup: Uruguay • NASCAR Championship: Bill Rexford • Wimbledon: Louise Brough Clapp and Budge Patty • U.S. Open: Margaret Osborne duPont and Arthur Larsen • World Figure Skating Championships: Aja Zanova (Czechoslovakia) and Dick Button (United States) • PGA Championship: Chandler Harper **CELEBRITY BIRTHS:** John Candy • Karen Carpenter • David Cassidy • Natalie Cole • Julius Erving • Morgan Fairchild • Peter Frampton • Peter Gabriel • Ed Harris • Christine Lahti • Jay Leno • Huey Lewis • William H. Macy • Dr. Phil McGraw • Bill Murray • Billy Ocean • Jane Pauley • Tom Petty • Nora Roberts • Tim Russert • Cybill Shepherd • Martin Short • Stevie Wonder **TRANSPORTATION:** Col. David C. Shilling makes the first nonstop transatlantic jet flight. Goodyear releases first self-repairing tires. Ignition key start switches replace push buttons.

TECHNOLOGY: Color TV begins broadcasting. Phonevision, the first pay-per-view service, becomes available.

INVENTIONS: Credit cards • disposable diapers • remote control • artificial snowmaking machine • leaf blower **NEW PRODUCTS:** DuPont's Orlon acrylic fiber • Xerox copying machines • Otis self-service elevators • Minute Rice • Sugar Pops • Clue board game • Fisher-Price's Little People • Magic 8-Ball **DISCOVERIES:** Richard Lawler performs the first successful kidney transplant. **FADS:** The mambo dance is imported from Cuba. Young men sport the D.A., or "ducktail," hairstyle. Charles Shultz's "Peanuts" comic strip and Mort Walker's "Beetle Bailey" begin publication. Saturday morning children's TV programming begins. Shirley Temple retires.

our

1

2

3

favorites

$

MILK
$0.82/gallon

GAS
$0.27/gallon

NEW HOME
$14,500

AVERAGE INCOME
$3,815/year

MINIMUM WAGE
$0.75/hour

FAMILY Milestones

WHERE WE LIVED: ....

....

....

JOBS WE WORKED OR YEAR IN SCHOOL: ....

....

....

CARS WE DROVE: ....

....

PEOPLE WE LOVED: ....

....

SONGS WE LOVED: ....

....

MOVIES WE LOVED: ....

....

TRIPS WE TOOK: ....

....

TECHNOLOGY WE BOUGHT: ....

....

MAJOR MILESTONES:

» Births: ....

....

» Graduations: ....

....

» Marriages: ....

....

» Deaths: ....

....

favorite memory...

....

....

....

....

....

1951

TOP NEWS STORIES: President Harry S. Truman relieves Gen. Douglas MacArthur of his military duties. 250,000 GIs are in Korea. Flooding in Kansas and Missouri leaves 200,000 homeless. **GOVERNMENT:** 22nd Amendment limits a president to two terms. United States begins testing nuclear devices with live troops. **MEMORABLE SONGS:** "Because of You" by Tony Bennett • "Be My Love" by Mario Lanza • "Cold, Cold Heart" by Tony Bennett • "Come On-A My House" by Rosemary Clooney • "Cry" by Johnnie Ray • "How High the Moon" by Les Paul & Mary Ford • "If" by Perry Como • "Sin" by Eddy Howard • "Too Young" by Nat King Cole • "Unforgettable" by Nat King Cole **MEMORABLE MOVIES:** *The African Queen* • *An American in Paris* • *The Day the Earth Stood Still* • *A Streetcar Named Desire* **SPORTS:** NFL Championship: Los Angeles Rams • World Series: New York Yankees • NBA Championship: Rochester Royals • Stanley Cup: Toronto Maple Leafs • NASCAR Championship: Herb Thomas • World Figure Skating Championships: Jeannette Altwegg (Great Britain) and Dick Button (United States) • PGA Championship: Sam Snead • Wimbledon: Doris Hart and Dick Savitt • U.S. Open: Maureen Connolly and Frank Sedgman **CELEBRITY BIRTHS:** Kristie Alley • Peabo Bryson • Lynda Carter • Phil Collins • Dale Earnhardt • Dan Fogelberg • Anjelica Huston • Michael Keaton • Rush Limbaugh • John Mellenkamp • Suze Orman • Sally Ride • Jane Seymour • Sting • Marc Summers • Luther Vandross • Robin Williams **TRANSPORTATION:** Charles F. Blair, Jr., makes the first solo flight across the North Pole. **TECHNOLOGY:** The first power-producing nuclear reactor goes on line. The first transcontinental TV broadcast is an address by Truman. **INVENTIONS:** White correction fluid • Universal Automatic Computer (UNIVAC) **NEW PRODUCTS:** Colorforms **DISCOVERIES:** First oral contraceptive is developed. **FADS:** *The Sea Around Us* by Rachel Carson begins the environmental movement. Teenage girls wear poodle skirts and saddle shoes.

CULTURE: Popular TV shows include *The Cisco Kid, I Love Lucy, The Red Skelton Show, The Roy Rogers Show, Search for Tomorrow, Superman, Watch Mr. Wizard*, and *Your Show of Shows*. Americans begin building personal bomb shelters. Hank Ketcham introduces "Dennis the Menace." J.D. Salinger writes *The Catcher in the Rye*.

our 1 2 3 favorites

MILK
$0.92/gallon

GAS
$0.27/gallon

NEW HOME
$16,000

AVERAGE INCOME
$4,194/year

MINIMUM WAGE
$0.75/hour

FAMILY
Milestones

WHERE WE LIVED: ....

....

....

JOBS WE WORKED OR YEAR IN SCHOOL: ....

....

....

CARS WE DROVE: ....

....

PEOPLE WE LOVED: ....

....

SONGS WE LOVED: ....

....

MOVIES WE LOVED: ....

....

TRIPS WE TOOK: ....

....

TECHNOLOGY WE BOUGHT: ....

....

MAJOR MILESTONES: ....

» Births: ....

....

» Graduations: ....

....

» Marriages: ....

....

» Deaths: ....

....

favorite memory...

....

....

....

....

....

1952

TOP NEWS STORY: The hydrogen bomb is exploded at Eniwetok. A polio epidemic afflicts 50,000 Americans. **GOVERNMENT:** Dwight D. Eishenhower and Richard M. Nixon are elected president and vice president. Richard Nixon makes his "Checkers" speech. Age requirement for naturalization drops to 18; declaration of intention becomes optional. **MEMORABLE SONGS:** "Delicado" by Percey Faith • "The Glow-Worm" by Mills Brothers • "Half As Much" by Rosemary Clooney • "Here in My Heart" by Al Martino • "High Noon (Do Not Forsake Me)" by Frankie Laine • "I Went to Your Wedding" by Patti Page • "Kiss of Fire" by Georgia Gibbs • "Wheel of Fortune" by Kay Starr • "Why Don't You Believe Me" by Joni James • "You Belong to Me" by Jo Stafford **MEMORABLE MOVIES:** *The Greatest Show on Earth* • *High Noon* • *Singin' in the Rain* **SPORTS:** NFL Championship: Detroit Lions • World Series: New York Yankees • Stanley Cup: Detroit Red Wings • NBA Championship: Minneapolis Lakers • NASCAR Championship: Tim Flock • Wimbledon: Maureen Connolly and Frank Sedgman • U.S. Open: Maureen Connolly and Frank Sedgman • World Figure Skating Championship: Jacqueline du Bief (France) and Dick Button (United States) • PGA Championship: Jim Turnesa **CELEBRITY BIRTHS:** Dan Aykroyd • Christine Baranski • Roseanne Barr • John Goodman • David Hasselhoff • Liam Neeson • Sharon Osbourne • David Petraeus • Annie Potts • Christopher Reeve • Isabella Rossellini • Mickey Rourke • George Strait • Patrick Swayze • Mr. T • John Tesh **TRANSPORTATION:** The number of diesel-electric trains surpasses steam locomotives. **TECHNOLOGY:** The first videotape is demonstrated.

INVENTIONS: Defibrillator • cardiac pacemaker • automotive airbag • bar codes

---

NEW PRODUCTS: Sony's pocket-sized transistor radios • paint-by-number kits • Mr. Potato Head • *Mad* magazine **DISCOVERIES:** Jonas Salk develops a polio vaccine. **FADS:** Kids wear beanies with propellers. Panty raids become popular on college campuses. **CULTURE:** A minister, a priest, and a rabbi approve Lucille Ball's TV pregnancy. Revised Standard Version of the Bible is published. The first Holiday Inn opens in Memphis, Tennessee. Popular TV shows are *The Adventures of Ozzie & Harriet*, *American Bandstand*, *Death Valley Days*, *Dragnet*, *I've Got a Secret*, and *The Today Show*.

our 1 2 3 favorites

$

MILK
$0.96/gallon

GAS
$0.27/gallon

NEW HOME
$16,800

AVERAGE INCOME
$4,457/year

MINIMUM WAGE
$0.75/hour

FAMILY
Milestones

WHERE WE LIVED: ....

....

....

JOBS WE WORKED OR YEAR IN SCHOOL: ....

....

....

CARS WE DROVE: ....

....

PEOPLE WE LOVED: ....

....

SONGS WE LOVED: ....

....

MOVIES WE LOVED: ....

....

TRIPS WE TOOK: ....

....

TECHNOLOGY WE BOUGHT: ....

....

MAJOR MILESTONES:

» Births: ....

....

» Graduations: ....

....

» Marriages: ....

....

» Deaths: ....

....

favorite memory:

....

....

....

....

1953

TOP NEWS STORY: A Korean armistice is signed; U.S. casualties total 25,604 dead. **GOVERNMENT:** Earl Warren becomes Chief Justice of the Supreme Court. The IRS is formed. **MEMORABLE SONGS:** "The Doggie in the Window" by Patti Page • "Don't Let the Stars Get In Your Eyes" by Perry Como • "I'm Walking Behind You" by Eddie Fisher • "Rags to Riches" by Tony Bennett • "St. George and the Dragonet" by Stan Freberg • "Song from Moulin Rouge" by Percy Faith • "That's Amore" by Dean Martin • "Till I Waltz Again With You" by Teresa Brewer • "Vaya Con Dios" by Les Paul & Mary Ford • "Your Cheatin' Heart" by Hank Williams **MEMORABLE MOVIES:** *From Here to Eternity* • *Gentlemen Prefer Blondes* • *Peter Pan* • *Roman Holiday* • *Shane* • *The War of the Worlds* **SPORTS:** NFL Championship: Detroit Lions • World Series: New York Yankees • NBA Championship: Minneapolis Lakers • Stanley Cup: Montreal Canadiens • NASCAR Championship: Herb Thomas • Wimbledon: Maureen Connolly and Vic Seixas • U.S. Open: Maureen Connolly and Tony Trabert • World Figure Skating Championship: Tenley Albright (United States) and Hayes Alan Jenkins (United States) • PGA Championship: Walter Burkemo **CELEBRITY BIRTHS:** Tim Allen • Kim Bassinger • Pat Benatar • Tony Blair • Michael Bolton • Pierce Brosnan • Danny Elfman • Emilio Estefan • Kathie Lee Gifford • Cyndi Lauper • John Malkovich • Rick Moranis • Mary Steenburgen **TRANSPORTATION:** Aston Martin's DB2/4, the first hatchback, goes into production. The first Chevrolet Corvette is built. **TECHNOLOGY:** The heart-lung machine is developed. Physicist Charles Townes develops the MASER, a device that produces coherent electromagnetic waves through amplification by stimulated emission. **INVENTIONS:** Marker pen • transistorized hearing aid

---

NEW PRODUCTS: TV dinners • instant iced tea • Sugar Smacks cereal • Matchbox Cars • Wiffle Ball • Playboy • TV Guide

---

DISCOVERIES: Alfred Kinsey publishes his study *Sexual Behavior in the Human Female*. Watson and Crick decode the DNA double helix. Apgar scale to determine the physical status of a newborn is developed. The discovery of REM sleep is first published. **FADS:** Bermuda shorts are promoted for men, toreador pants for women. **CULTURE:** L. Ron Hubbard founds the Church of Scientology. Meteorologists give women's names to hurricanes. Charlie Chaplin is banned from the United States. KUHI is the first educational TV station. Popular TV shows include *Flash Gordon*, *General Electric Theatre*, *The Jackie Gleason Show*, *The Loretta Young Show*, and *Romper Room*.

our 1 2 3 favorites

$

MILK
$0.94/gallon

GAS
$0.29/gallon

NEW HOME
$17,400

AVERAGE INCOME
$4,706/year

MINIMUM WAGE
$0.75/hour

FAMILY Milestones

WHERE WE LIVED: ....

....

....

JOBS WE WORKED OR YEAR IN SCHOOL:

....

....

CARS WE DROVE: ....

....

PEOPLE WE LOVED: ....

....

SONGS WE LOVED: ....

....

MOVIES WE LOVED: ....

....

TRIPS WE TOOK: ....

....

TECHNOLOGY WE BOUGHT: ....

....

MAJOR MILESTONES: ....

» Births: ....

....

» Graduations: ....

....

» Marriages: ....

....

» Deaths: ....

....

favorite memory...

....

....

....

....

....

19 54

TOP NEWS STORIES: Supreme Court outlaws segregation in public schools in Brown v. Board of Education of Topeka, Kansas. Puerto Rican nationalists shoot five Congressmen. The Iwo Jima Memorial Monument is dedicated in Washington, DC.

GOVERNMENT: U.S. Air Force Academy is established. U.S. Senate votes to condemn Joseph McCarthy for "conduct that tends to bring the Senate into dishonor and dispute." **MEMORABLE SONGS:** "Hey There" by Rosemary Clooney • "I Need You Now" by Eddie Fisher • "Little Things Mean a Lot" by Kitty Kallen • "Mr. Sandman" by Chordettes • "Oh! My Papa" by Eddie Fisher • "Secret Love" by Doris Day • "Sh-Boom" by Crew-Cuts • "This Ole House" by Rosemary Clooney • "Wanted" by Perry Como **MEMORA-BLE MOVIES:** *The Bridges at Toko-Ri* • *The Caine Mutiny* • *Dial M for Murder* • *On the Waterfront* • *Sabrina* • *A Star is Born* • *White Christmas* **SPORTS:** NFL Championship: Cleveland Browns • World Series: New York Giants • Stanley Cup: Detroit Red Wings • NBA Championship: Minneapolis Lakers • World Cup: West Germany • Wimbledon: Maureen Connolly and Jaroslav Drobny• U.S. Open: Doris Hart and Victor Seixas • NASCAR Championship: Lee Petty • World Figure Skating Championship: Gundi Busch (Germany) and Hayes Alan Jenkins (United States) • PGA Championship: Chick Harbert **CELEBRITY BIRTHS:** Scott Bakula • James Belushi • Christie Brinkley • James Cameron • Jackie Chan • Tony Dorsett • Chris Evert • Ron Howard • Annie Lennox • Ray Liotta • Michael Moore • Walter Payton • Dennis Quaid • Al Roker • Rene Russo • Jerry Seinfeld • John Travolta • Denzel Washington • Oprah Winfrey **TRANSPORTATION:** USS *Nautilus* is the first atomic submarine. Chevrolet Corvette goes on sale. Boeing releases the 707. **TECHNOLOGY:** RCA makes color TVs. **INVENTIONS:** Photovoltaic cells • silicon transistors **NEW PRODUCTS:** *Sports Illustrated* • Robert the Robot toy **DISCOVERIES:** The first successful kidney transplant occurs. **FADS:** The cha-cha dance becomes popular. Fess Parker starts the Davy Crockett craze. **CULTURE:** Children are inoculated with Salk's polio vaccine. President Dwight D. Eisenhower changes the Pledge of Allegiance to include the words "under God." Popular TV shows are *Father Knows Best*, *Lassie*, *People Are Funny*, *This Is Your Lif*e, *The Tonight Show*, and the *Walt Disney Show*. Marilyn Monroe marries Joe DiMaggio. The last radio episode of *The Lone Ranger* airs. The first Burger King opens.

our 1 2 3 favorites

$

MILK
$0.92/gallon

GAS
$0.29/gallon

NEW HOME
$17,500

AVERAGE INCOME
$4,684/year

MINIMUM WAGE
$0.75/hour

FAMILY
Milestones

WHERE WE LIVED: ....

....

....

JOBS WE WORKED OR YEAR IN SCHOOL:

....

....

CARS WE DROVE: ....

....

PEOPLE WE LOVED: ....

....

SONGS WE LOVED: ....

....

MOVIES WE LOVED: ....

....

TRIPS WE TOOK: ....

....

TECHNOLOGY WE BOUGHT: ....

....

MAJOR MILESTONES:

» Births: ....

....

» Graduations: ....

....

» Marriages: ....

....

» Deaths: ....

....

favorite memory

....

....

....

....

....

1955

TOP NEWS STORIES: Argentina ousts dictator Juan Perón. Rosa Parks refuses to sit at the back of the bus, breaking a Montgomery, Alabama, segregated seating law and leading to a 381-day black boycott of the Montgomery bus system. Hurricane Diane hits northeastern United States, killing more than 200 and causing more than $1 billion in damage. **GOVERNMENT:** U.S. Air Force Academy opens. The AFL and CIO merge. **MEMORABLE SONGS:** "Autumn Leaves" by Roger Williams • "The Ballad of Davy Crockett" by Bill Hayes • "Love and Marriage" by Frank Sinatra • "Love Is a Many-Splendored Thing" by Four Aces • "Maybellene" by Chuck Berry • "Rock Around the Clock" by Bill Haley & His Comets • "Sixteen Tons" by Tennessee Ernie Ford • "The Yellow Rose of Texas" by Mitch Miller **MEMORABLE MOVIES:** *Blackboard Jungle* • *East of Eden* • *Lady and the Tramp* • *Mister Roberts* • *Rebel Without a Cause* • *The Seven Year Itch* **SPORTS:** NFL Championship: Cleveland Browns • World Series: Brooklyn Dodgers • Stanley Cup: Detroit Red Wings • NBA Championship: Syracuse Nationals • NASCAR Championship: Tim Flock • Wimbledon: Louise Brough Clapp and Tony Trabert • U.S. Open: Doris Hart and Tony Trabert • World Figure Skating Championships: Tenley Albright (United States) and Hayes Alan Jenkins (United States) • PGA Championship: Doug Ford

CELEBRITY BIRTHS: Dana Carvey • Kevin Costner • Willem Dafoe • Peter Gallagher • Bill Gates • Kelsey Grammer • Whoopi Goldberg • Billy Idol • Steve Jobs • Barbara Kingsolver • Howie Mandel • Reba McEntire • Bill Nye • Bill Paxton • Maria Shriver • Jimmy Smits • Billy Bob Thornton • Eddie Van Halen • Bruce Willis • Debra Winger

TRANSPORTATION: Ford Thunderbird is introduced. **TECHNOLOGY:** Severo Ochoa at NYU synthesizes DNA- and RNA-like molecules. Albert Sabin develops an oral polio vaccine. **INVENTIONS:** Respirator • music synthesizer • artificial diamond • fiber optics • hard disk drive **NEW PRODUCTS:** Crest toothpaste • Special K cereal **FADS:** Pink suddenly appears in menswear. Automobile stuffing becomes popular on college campuses. **CULTURE:** The Presbyterian Church approves ordination of women ministers. Rock and roll music is declared "immoral." Disneyland opens in Anaheim, California. H&R Block and Kentucky Fried Chicken are founded. James Dean dies in a car wreck. Jim Henson creates Kermit the Frog. Popular TV shows include *Captain Kangaroo*, *Gunsmoke*, *The Honeymooners*, *The Lawrence Welk Show*, and *Sheena, Queen of the Jungle*.

our favorites

MILK
$0.92/gallon

GAS
$0.29/gallon

NEW HOME
$17,600

AVERAGE INCOME
$4,962/year

MINIMUM WAGE
$0.75/hour

FAMILY Milestones

WHERE WE LIVED: ....

....

....

JOBS WE WORKED OR YEAR IN SCHOOL: ....

....

....

CARS WE DROVE: ....

....

PEOPLE WE LOVED: ....

....

SONGS WE LOVED: ....

....

MOVIES WE LOVED: ....

....

TRIPS WE TOOK: ....

....

TECHNOLOGY WE BOUGHT: ....

....

MAJOR MILESTONES: ....

» Births: ....

....

» Graduations: ....

....

» Marriages: ....

....

» Deaths: ....

....

favorite memory. ....

....

....

....

....

....

19**56**

TOP NEWS STORIES: The last Union Army veteran from the Civil War, Albert Woolson, dies at age 109. The *Andrea Doria* sinks off Nantucket Island. "Hiroshima Maidens" receive plastic surgery for radiation burns. **GOVERNMENT:** Dwight D. Eisenhower and Richard Nixon are re-elected president and vice president. **MEMORABLE SONGS:** "Blueberry Hill" by Fats Domino • "The Great Pretender" by The Platters • "Heartbreak Hotel" by Elvis Presley • "Hound Dog" by Elvis Presley • "Lisbon Antigua" by Nelson Riddle • "Love Me Tender" by Elvis Presley • "Memories Are Made of This" by Dean Martin • "The Poor People of Paris" by Les Baxter • "Singing the Blues" by Guy Mitchell • "The Wayward Wind" by Gogi Grant **MEMORABLE MOVIES:** *Around the World in Eighty Days* • *The King and I* • *The Forbidden Planet* • *The Ten Commandments* **SPORTS:** NFL Championship: New York Giants • World Series: New York Yankees • Stanley Cup: Montreal Canadiens • NBA Championship: Philadelphia Warriors • NASCAR Championship: Buck Baker • Wimbledon: Shirley Fry and Lew Hoad • U.S. Open: Shirley Fry and Ken Rosewall • World Figure Skating Championship: Carol Heiss (United States) and Hayes Alan Jenkins (United States) • PGA Championship: Jack Burke Jr. **CELEBRITY BIRTHS:** Larry Bird • David Caruso • Kim Cattrall • David Copperfield • Geena Davis • Dana Delany • Bo Derek • Carrie Fisher • Andy García • Mel Gibson • Tom Hanks • Chris Isaak • Dale Jarrett • Nathan Lane • Bill Maher • Maureen McCormick • Mimi Rogers • Sela Ward • Rita Wilson • Paula Zahn **TRANSPORTATION:** The Interstate Highway program is authorized. United States tests the first aerial hydrogen bomb over Namu islet, Bikini Atoll. **TECHNOLOGY:** The first transatlantic telephone cable becomes operational. **INVENTIONS:** The Polaris missile is developed. Felix Wankel develops the rotary internal combustion engine. **NEW PRODUCTS:** Play-Doh • Yahtzee dice game • Stainless steel razor blades • Pampers • Comet cleanser

---

DISCOVERIES: The subatomic neutrino is observed. The DNA molecule is first photographed.

FADS: Crew cuts and flat tops are popular haircuts. Short shorts become acceptable. **CULTURE:** Methodist Church abolishes racial separation in its churches. Midas Muffler opens. Ringling Brothers & Barnum and Bailey Circus folds. *My Fair Lady* with Julie Andrews is on Broadway. Actress Grace Kelly marries Prince Rainier II of Monaco. 54 million watch Elvis on *The Ed Sullivan Show*. Popular TV shows include *As the World Turns*, *Broken Arrow*, *Dick Powell's Zane Grey Theatre*, and *The Dinah Shore Chevy Show*.

our

1

2

3

favorites

$

MILK
$0.97/gallon

GAS
$0.30/gallon

NEW HOME
$17,800

AVERAGE INCOME
$5,341/year

MINIMUM WAGE
$1/hour

FAMILY Milestones

WHERE WE LIVED: ....

....

....

JOBS WE WORKED OR YEAR IN SCHOOL:

....

....

CARS WE DROVE: ....

....

PEOPLE WE LOVED: ....

....

SONGS WE LOVED: ....

....

MOVIES WE LOVED: ....

....

TRIPS WE TOOK: ....

....

TECHNOLOGY WE BOUGHT: ....

....

MAJOR MILESTONES:

» Births: ....

....

» Graduations: ....

....

» Marriages: ....

....

» Deaths: ....

....

1957

TOP NEWS STORIES: Federal troops desegregate Central High School in Little Rock, Arkansas. New York's "Mad Bomber" is arrested. Russia launches Sputnik I, the first earth-orbiting satellite. **GOVERNMENT:** A civil rights bill passes Congress. President Dwight D. Eisenhower extends the Truman Doctrine to cover the Middle East.

MEMORABLE SONGS: "All Shook Up" by Elvis Presley • "At the Hop" by Danny and the Juniors • "Diana" by Paul Anka • "Great Balls of Fire" by Jerry Lee Lewis • "Jailhouse Rock" by Elvis Presley • "Love Letters in the Sand" by Pat Boone • "Peggy Sue" by Buddy Holly • "Wake Up Little Susie" by The Everly Brothers

MEMORABLE MOVIES: *An Affair to Remember* • *Bridge on the River Kwai* • *The Incredible Shrinking Man* • *Jailhouse Rock* **SPORTS:** NFL Championship: Detroit Lions • World Series: Milwaukee Braves • NBA Championship: Boston Celtics • Stanley Cup: Montreal Canadiens • NASCAR Championship: Buck Baker • Wimbledon: Althea Gibson and Lew Hoad • U.S. Open: Althea Gibson and Malcolm Anderson • World Figure Skating Championship: Carol Heiss (United States) and David Jenkins (United States) • PGA Championship: Lionel Hebert **CELEBRITY BIRTHS:** Katie Couric • Fran Drescher • Gloria Estefan • Kevin Eubanks • Melanie Griffith • Steve Harvey • Matt Lauer • Dennis Leary • Spike Lee • Bernie Mac • Ray Romano • Paul Reiser • Payne Stewart • Vanna White **TRANSPORTATION:** Ford Motor Company introduces the ill-fated Edsel. Chevrolet Bel Air goes on sale, becoming an American classic and one of the most popular cars in history. First round-the-world nonstop jet plane flight occurs. **TECHNOLOGY:** An intercontinental ballistic missile (ICBM) is successfully tested. American scientists urge ban on nuclear weapons. The first large nuclear power plant goes on line. **INVENTIONS:** Internal pacemaker • stereo recording **NEW PRODUCTS:** Spandex **DISCOVERIES:** Alick Isaacs and Jean Lindemann invent interferon. **FADS:** Black leather jackets are popular with teenage boys. Plaid sport jackets are introduced for men. The sack dress is introduced. Wham-O introduces the Hula Hoop and Frisbee. **CULTURE:** Jimmy Hoffa becomes head of the Teamsters union. *West Side Story* musical debuts on Broadway. Popular TV shows include *The Gumby Show*, *Have Gun Will Travel*, *Leave it to Beaver*, *Perry Mason*, *The Real McCoys*, *Twenty One*, and *Wagon Train*.

our 1 2 3 favorites

$

MILK
$1/gallon

GAS
$0.31/gallon

NEW HOME
$18,000

AVERAGE INCOME
$5,443/year

MINIMUM WAGE
$1/hour

FAMILY Milestones

WHERE WE LIVED: ....

....

....

JOBS WE WORKED OR YEAR IN SCHOOL: ....

....

....

CARS WE DROVE: ....

....

PEOPLE WE LOVED: ....

....

SONGS WE LOVED: ....

....

MOVIES WE LOVED: ....

....

TRIPS WE TOOK: ....

....

TECHNOLOGY WE BOUGHT: ....

....

MAJOR MILESTONES:

» Births: ....

....

» Graduations: ....

....

» Marriages: ....

....

» Deaths: ....

....

favorite memory...

....

....

....

....

....

1958

TOP NEWS STORIES: 87 children die in a fire at Our Lady of the Angels School in Chicago. Charles Starkweather and his girlfriend are arrested after a killing spree. U.S. troops deploy to Lebanon. **GOVERNMENT:** Congress passes U.S. National Defense Education Act to promote math and science. NASA and the FAA are established. **MEMORABLE SONGS:** "All I Have to Do Is Dream" by Everly Brothers • "The Chipmunk Song" by David Seville/The Chipmunks • "It's All in the Game" by Tommy Edwards • "Johnny B. Goode" by Chuck Berry • "The Purple People Eater" by Sheb Wooley • "Smoke Gets in Your Eyes" by The Platters • "Tequila" by Champs • "Tom Dooley" by The Kingston Trio • "Volare" by Domenico Modugno • "Yakety Yak" by The Coasters **MEMORABLE MOVIES:** *Cat on a Hot Tin Roof* • *Gigi* • *Touch of Evil* • *Vertigo* **SPORTS:** NFL Championship: Baltimore Colts • World Series: New York Yankees • NBA Championship: St. Louis Hawks • Stanley Cup: Montreal Canadiens • World Cup: Brazil • Wimbledon: Althea Gibson and Ashley Cooper • U.S. Open: Althea Gibson and Ashley Cooper • World Figure Skating Championships: Carol Heiss (United States) and David Jenkins (United States) • PGA Championship: Dow Finsterwald • NASCAR Championship: Lee Petty **CELEBRITY BIRTHS:** Kevin Bacon • Alec Baldwin • Angela Bassett • Annette Bening • Andrea Bocelli • Tim Burton • Drew Carey • Mary Chapin Carpenter • Jamie Lee Curtis • Ellen DeGeneres • Scott Hamilton • Patricia Heaton • Holly Hunter • Michael Jackson • Joan Jett • Andie MacDowell • Madonna • Gary Oldman • Michelle Pfeiffer • Prince • Sharon Stone **TRANSPORTATION:** USS *Nautilus* makes the first undersea crossing of North Pole. Boeing 707 goes into service. First transatlantic jet passenger service starts with a New York to London route. Chevrolet Impala introduced. **TECHNOLOGY:** Ultrasound is first used to examine an unborn fetus. United States launches its first satellite, Explorer I. NASA starts Project Mercury, aimed at putting a man in space within two years. **INVENTIONS:** Skateboard • laser • integrated circuit **NEW PRODUCTS:** Sweet'N Low • Americard (now Visa) • American Express card **DISCOVERIES:** The Van Allen radiation belts are discovered.

FADS: The "beatnik" look calls for dark clothes.

CULTURE: The first Pizza Hut opens in Kansas City. Popular TV shows are *77 Sunset Strip*, *The Donna Reed Show*, *Huckleberry Hound*, *Maverick*, *Naked City*, and *The Rifleman*. The Liz Taylor-Eddie Fisher-Debbie Reynolds love triangle is a Hollywood scandal. *Billboard* debuts its Hot 100 chart.

our 1 2 3 favorites

$

MILK
$1/gallon

GAS
$0.30/gallon

NEW HOME
$18,200

AVERAGE INCOME
$5,556/year

MINIMUM WAGE
$1/hour

FAMILY
Milestones

WHERE WE LIVED: ....

....

....

JOBS WE WORKED OR YEAR IN SCHOOL: ....

....

....

CARS WE DROVE: ....

....

PEOPLE WE LOVED: ....

....

SONGS WE LOVED: ....

....

MOVIES WE LOVED: ....

....

TRIPS WE TOOK: ....

....

TECHNOLOGY WE BOUGHT: ....

....

MAJOR MILESTONES: ....

» Births: ....

....

» Graduations: ....

....

» Marriages: ....

....

» Deaths: ....

....

favorite memory.

....

....

....

....

....

19**59**

TOP NEWS STORIES: Vice President Nixon and Soviet Premier Khrushchev engage in a "kitchen debate" in Moscow. Walter Williams, the last Confederate soldier, dies at age 117. Buddy Holly, Ritchie Valens, and the Big Bopper die in a plane crash. Fidel Castro assumes power in Cuba.

GOVERNMENT: Alaska and Hawaii become 49th and 50th states. NASA selects the first seven U.S. astronauts. **MEMORABLE SONGS:** "The Battle of New Orleans" by Johnny Horton • "Dream Lover" by Bobby Darin • "Heartaches By the Number" by Guy Mitchell • "Lonely Boy" by Paul Anka • "Mack the Knife" by Bobby Darin • "Stagger Lee" by Lloyd Price • "Venus" by Frankie Avalon **MEMORABLE MOVIES:** *Ben-Hur* • *The Diary of Anne Frank* • *Gidget* • *North by Northwest* • *Sleeping Beauty* • *Some Like It Hot* **SPORTS:** NFL Championship: Baltimore Colts • World Series: Los Angeles Dodgers • NBA Championship: Boston Celtics • Stanley Cup: Montreal Canadiens • World Figure Skating Championship: Carol Heiss (United States) and David Jenkins (United States) • PGA Championship: Bob Rosburg • NASCAR Championship: Lee Petty • Wimbledon: Maria Bueno and Alex Olmedo • U.S. Open: Maria Bueno and Neale Fraser **CELEBRITY BIRTHS:** Bryan Adams • Tom Arnold • Rupert Everett • Allison Janney • Val Kilmer • John McEnroe • Jim Nantz • David Hyde Pierce • Mackenzie Phillips • Kevin Spacey • Emma Thompson • Tracey Ullman • "Weird Al" Yankovic **TRANSPORTATION:** American Motors introduces the Rambler to compete with small foreign cars. The St. Lawrence Seaway opens. **TECHNOLOGY:** The first weather satellite, Vanguard 2, launches. **INVENTIONS:** Shoulder seat belt

NEW PRODUCTS: Tang • pantyhose • Barbie doll • Troll doll • Chatty Cathy doll

DISCOVERIES: USSR's Lunik II probe reaches the moon. **FADS:** Telephone-booth-stuffing is the rage on college campuses. **CULTURE:** Berry Gordy founds Motown Records. Popular TV shows include *Bonanza, Rawhide, Rocky and His Friends, The Twilight Zone,* and *The Untouchables.* The "great quiz show scandal" exposes advance coaching of contestants. Annual Grammy Awards ceremony begins.

our

1

2

3

favorites

$

MILK
$1.01/gallon

GAS
$0.30/gallon

NEW HOME
$18,400

AVERAGE INCOME
$5,976/year

MINIMUM WAGE
$1/hour

FAMILY Milestones

WHERE WE LIVED: ....

....

....

JOBS WE WORKED OR YEAR IN SCHOOL: ....

....

....

CARS WE DROVE: ....

....

PEOPLE WE LOVED: ....

....

SONGS WE LOVED: ....

....

MOVIES WE LOVED: ....

....

TRIPS WE TOOK: ....

....

TECHNOLOGY WE BOUGHT: ....

....

MAJOR MILESTONES: ....

» Births: ....

....

» Graduations: ....

....

» Marriages: ....

....

» Deaths: ....

....

19 60

TOP NEWS STORIES: President Dwight D. Eisenhower warns against the "military-industrial-complex" while John F. Kennedy campaigns to close the "missile gap." The Soviets shoot down a U-2 spy plane. African-Americans sit-in at lunch counters to force desegregation. **GOVERNMENT:** John F. Kennedy and Lyndon B. Johnson are elected president and vice president.

CENSUS RESULTS: U.S. population is 179,245,000. More than 2.5 million immigrants entered the United States in the previous decade.

MEMORABLE SONGS: "Are You Lonesome Tonight?" by Elvis Presley • "Cathy's Clown" by The Everly Brothers • "Georgia on My Mind" by Ray Charles • "It's Now or Never" by Elvis Presley • "Itsy Bitsy Teenie Weenie Yellow Polka Dot Bikini" by Brian Hyland • "Running Bear" by Johnny Preston • "Save the Last Dance for Me" by Drifters • "Teen Angel" by Mark Dinning • "The Twist" by Chubby Checker **MEMORABLE MOVIES:** The Apartment • The Magnificent Seven • Psycho • Spartacus **SPORTS:** NFL Championship: Philadelphia Eagles • World Series: Pittsburgh Pirates • NBA Championship: Boston Celtics • World Figure Skating Championships: Carol Heiss (United States) and Alain Giletti (France) • PGA Championship: Jay Hebert • NASCAR Championship: Rex White • Wimbledon: Maria Bueno and Neale Fraser • U.S. Open: Darlene Hard and Neale Fraser **CELEBRITY BIRTHS:** Antonio Banderas • Bono • David Duchovny • Colin Firth • Amy Grant • Hugh Grant • Jennifer Grey • Daryl Hannah • John F. Kennedy Jr. • Greg Louganis • Jane Lynch • Julianne Moore • Sean Penn • Cal Ripkin Jr. • Kristin Scott Thomas **TRANSPORTATION:** The USS Triton completes the first undersea circumnavigation of the globe. The United States has more than 2.17 million miles of surfaced road. **TECHNOLOGY:** Tiros I, a weather satellite, and Echo I, the first communications satellite, launch. **INVENTIONS:** first working laser **NEW PRODUCTS:** Soft drinks in aluminum cans • Hi-Ho! Cherry-O game • Etch-a-Sketch **DISCOVERIES:** Quasars are discovered. **FADS:** Jackie Kennedy becomes a model of good taste in fashion. Pierced ears become acceptable. **CULTURE:** An oral contraceptive, "the Pill," is marketed. Pat Robertson founds the Christian Broadcasting Network. Harper Lee publishes To Kill a Mockingbird. 73 million people watch Nixon and Kennedy debate on TV. Popular TV shows are The Andy Griffith Show, The Flintstones, and My Three Sons. 90 percent of U.S. homes have a TV set. The Playboy Bunny debuts. John Coltrane becomes the voice of jazz's New Wave movement.

our 1 2 3 favorites

$

MILK
$1.04/gallon

GAS
$0.31/gallon

NEW HOME
$18,500

AVERAGE INCOME
$6,227/year

MINIMUM WAGE
$1/hour

FAMILY
Milestones

WHERE WE LIVED: ....

....

....

JOBS WE WORKED OR YEAR IN SCHOOL: ....

....

....

CARS WE DROVE: ....

....

PEOPLE WE LOVED: ....

....

SONGS WE LOVED: ....

....

MOVIES WE LOVED: ....

....

TRIPS WE TOOK: ....

....

TECHNOLOGY WE BOUGHT: ....

....

MAJOR MILESTONES: ....

» Births: ....

....

» Graduations: ....

....

» Marriages: ....

....

» Deaths: ....

....

favorite memory

....

....

....

....

1961

TOP NEWS STORIES: Alan Shepard is the first American in space. President John F. Kennedy challenges the Soviets to a race to the moon. After the failed "Bay of Pigs" invasion, Washington severs relations with Cuba. **GOVERNMENT:** President Kennedy creates the Peace Corps. **MEMORABLE SONGS:** "Blue Moon" by Marcels • "Calcutta" by Lawrence Welk • "I Fall to Pieces" by Patsy Cline • "The Lion Sleeps Tonight" by Tokens • "Moon River" by Andy Williams • "Please Mr. Postman" by the Marvelettes • "Runaround Sue" by Dion • "Runaway" by Del Shannon • "Surrender" by Elvis Presley • "Tossin' and Turnin'" by Bobby Lewis • "Will You Love Me Tomorrow" by the Shirelles

MEMORABLE MOVIES: *Breakfast at Tiffany's • El Cid • One Hundred and One Dalmations • The Parent Trap • West Side Story*

SPORTS: NFL Championship: Green Bay Packers • World Series: New York Yankees • NBA Championship: Boston Celtics • Stanley Cup: Chicago Blackhawks • NASCAR Championship: Ned Jarrett • PGA Championship: Jerry Barber • Wimbledon: Angela Mortimer Barrett and Rod Laver • U.S. Open: Darlene Hard and Roy Emerson **CELEBRITY BIRTHS:** George Clooney • Ann Coulter • Billy Ray Cyrus • Enya • Michael J. Fox • Wayne Gretzky • Woody Harrelson • Heather Locklear • George Lopez • Julia Louis-Dreyfus • Eddie Murphy • Barack Obama • Dennis Rodman • Meg Ryan • Diana Spencer (Princess of Wales) • Isaiah Thomas • Bob Woodruff **TRANSPORTATION:** The Pontiac Tempest is *Motor Trend* magazine's Car of the Year. The 1961 Continental is the first American car with a 24,000-mile or two-year warranty. **TECHNOLOGY:** Biofeedback, a form of alternative medicine, is developed. **INVENTIONS:** IBM Selectric typewriter • intrauterine device contraceptive **NEW PRODUCTS:** acetaminophen • electric toothbrush • Slip 'N Slide **DISCOVERIES:** Scientists link smoking to heart disease. The drug thalidomide is found to cause birth defects. **FADS:** "Greasy kid stuff" (hair product) is out of style. The beehive hairdo is popular, as are yo-yos. **CULTURE:** President Kennedy increases U.S. military presence in Vietnam. The National Council of Churches endorses birth control. Joseph Heller publishes *Catch 22*. Bob Dylan begins his recording career. Popular TV shows include *Ben Casey*, *The Dick Van Dyke Show*, *Mr. Ed*, and *Wide World of Sports*. The FCC chairman calls TV "a vast wasteland."

our
1
2
3
favorites

$

MILK
$1.05/gallon

GAS
$0.31/gallon

NEW HOME
$18,800

AVERAGE INCOME
$6,471/year

MINIMUM WAGE
$1.15/hour

FAMILY Milestones

WHERE WE LIVED: ....

....

....

JOBS WE WORKED OR YEAR IN SCHOOL: ....

....

....

CARS WE DROVE: ....

....

PEOPLE WE LOVED: ....

....

SONGS WE LOVED: ....

....

MOVIES WE LOVED: ....

....

TRIPS WE TOOK: ....

....

TECHNOLOGY WE BOUGHT: ....

....

MAJOR MILESTONES: ....

» Births: ....

....

» Graduations: ....

....

» Marriages: ....

....

» Deaths: ....

....

favorite memory...

....

....

....

....

....

19 62

TOP NEWS STORIES: The Cuban Missile Crisis brings the United States and the Soviet Union to the brink of war. Marilyn Monroe dies from a drug overdose. John Glenn is the first American to orbit the earth. **GOVERNMENT:** U.S. advisors in Vietnam are allowed to return fire. **MEMORABLE SONGS:** "Big Girls Don't Cry" by the Four Seasons • "Breaking Up is Hard to Do" by Neil Sedaka • "Can't Help Falling in Love" by Elvis Presley • "Duke of Earl" by Gene Chandler • "Hey! Baby" by Bruce Channel • "I Can't Stop Loving You" by Ray Charles • "Peppermint Twist" by Joey Dee and the Starliters • "Return to Sender" by Elvis Presley • "Sherry" by Four Seasons • "Telestar" by the Tornadoes **MEMORABLE MOVIES:** *Dr. No* • *How the West Was Won* • *Lawrence of Arabia* • *The Manchurian Candidate* • *The Miracle Worker* • *What Ever Happened to Baby Jane?* **SPORTS:** NFL Championship: Green Bay Packers • World Series: New York Yankees • Stanley Cup: Toronto Maple Leafs • NBA Championship: Boston Celtics • World Figure Skating Championship: Sjoukje Dijkstra (Netherlands) and Donald Jackson (Canada) • NASCAR Championship: Joe Weatherly • Wimbledon: Karen Hantze Susman and Rod Laver • U.S. Open: Margaret Court and Rod Laver • PGA Championship: Gary Player **CELEBRITY BIRTHS:** Clint Black • Jon Bon Jovi • Matthew Broderick • Steve Carell • Jim Carrey • Steven Curtis Chapman • Marcia Cross • Tom Cruise • Joan Cusack • Anthony Edwards • Patrick Ewing • Craig Ferguson • Jodie Foster • Evander Holyfield • Felicity Huffman • Steve Irwin • Jackie Joyner-Kersee • Demi Moore • Rosie O'Donnell • Kelly Preston • Axl Rose • Mike Rowe • Wesley Snipes • Darryl Strawberry • Herschel Walker **TRANSPORTATION:** *Motor Trend* names Buick Special its Car of the Year. Buick introduces the Skylark. Telestar I transmits live telecasts between the United States and Britain. Mariner II, the first interplanetary probe, reaches Venus.

TECHNOLOGY: Eye surgery is performed using a laser.

INVENTIONS: LED • glucose meter **NEW PRODUCTS:** Diet-Rite, the first diet soda **DISCOVERIES:** Unimation Inc. introduces the first industrial robot. **FADS:** Teenage boys wear pointy shoes with Cuban heels. **CULTURE:** César Chavez leads the National Farm Workers Association in California. The first Kmart and Wal-Mart stores open. Popular TV shows include *Beany and Cecil*, *The Beverly Hillbillies*, *McHale's Navy*, *The Merv Griffin Show*, and *The Tonight Show* starring Johnny Carson.

our 1 2 3 favorites

$

MILK
$1.04/gallon

GAS
$0.31/gallon

NEW HOME
$19,000

AVERAGE INCOME
$6,670/year

MINIMUM WAGE
$1.15/hour

FAMILY Milestones

WHERE WE LIVED: ....

....

....

JOBS WE WORKED OR YEAR IN SCHOOL:

....

....

CARS WE DROVE: ....

....

PEOPLE WE LOVED: ....

....

SONGS WE LOVED: ....

....

MOVIES WE LOVED: ....

....

TRIPS WE TOOK: ....

....

TECHNOLOGY WE BOUGHT: ....

....

MAJOR MILESTONES: ....

» Births: ....

....

» Graduations: ....

....

» Marriages: ....

....

» Deaths: ....

....

favorite memory...

....

....

....

....

....

19 63

TOP NEWS STORIES: John F. Kennedy is assassinated in Dallas, Texas. The USS *Thresher* sinks with all men aboard. 200,000 march on Washington to demonstrate for civil rights. NACCP leader Medgar Evers is murdered.

GOVERNMENT: Lyndon B. Johnson becomes president. U.S. Supreme Court rules that accused criminals have the right to free counsel. U.S. Clean Air Act becomes law. **MEMORABLE SONGS:** "He's So Fine" by Chiffons • "Hey Paula" by Paul and Paula • "It's My Party" by Lesley Gore • "I Will Follow Him" by Little Peggy March • "Louie Louie" by Kingsmen • "My Boyfriend's Back" by Angels • "Puff (The Magic Dragon)" by Peter, Paul, and Mary • "Ring of Fire" by Johnny Cash • "She Loves You" by The Beatles • "Surfin' U.S.A." by The Beach Boys • "Walk Like a Man" by The Four Seasons **MEMORABLE MOVIES:** *The Birds* • *Cleopatra* • *Flipper* • *From Russia With Love* • *The Great Escape* • *The Nutty Professor* • *The Pink Panther* **SPORTS:** NFL Championship: Chicago Bears • World Series: Los Angeles Dodgers • NBA Championship: Boston Celtics • Stanley Cup: Toronto Maple Leafs • World Figure Skating Championship: Sjoukje Dijkstra (Netherlands) and Donald McPherson (Canada) • PGA Championship: Jack Nicklaus • NASCAR Championship: Joe Weatherly • Wimbledon: Margaret Court and Chuck McKinley • U.S. Open: Maria Bueno and Rafael Osuna **CELEBRITY BIRTHS:** Charles Barkley • Brian Boitano • Benjamin Bratt • James Denton • Johnny Depp • Whitney Houston • Helen Hunt • Michael Jordan • Greg Kinnear • Lisa Kudrow • Karl Malone • Richard Marx • Mark McGuire • Mike Myers • Conan O'Brien • Hakeem Olajuwon • Brad Pitt • John Stamos • Quentin Tarantino • Vanessa Williams **TRANSPORTATION:** Rambler is *Motor Trend*'s Car of the Year. Other popular cars are Buick Riviera and Studebaker Avanti. **TECHNOLOGY:** Digital Equipment Corporation introduces a successful minicomputer. **INVENTIONS:** Plasma displays • computer mouse • BASIC computer programming language **NEW PRODUCTS:** Instamatic camera • Touch-Tone phone • Easy-Bake Oven • Mouse Trap game **DISCOVERIES:** The first lung and liver transplants are performed. **FADS:** Hootenannies become popular. Ratfink by Ed "Big Daddy" Roth • Troll dolls **CULTURE:** New Hampshire institutes a state lottery to raise money for education. The Catholic Church approves vernacular languages for Mass. Betty Friedan writes *The Feminine Mystique* and Maurice Sendak writes *Where the Wild Things Are*.

our

1

2

3

favorites

$

MILK
$1.04/gallon

GAS
$0.30/gallon

NEW HOME
$19,300

AVERAGE INCOME
$6,998/year

MINIMUM WAGE
$1.25/hour

FAMILY Milestones

WHERE WE LIVED: ....

....

....

JOBS WE WORKED OR YEAR IN SCHOOL: ......

....

....

CARS WE DROVE: ....

....

PEOPLE WE LOVED: ....

....

SONGS WE LOVED: ....

....

MOVIES WE LOVED: ....

....

TRIPS WE TOOK: ....

....

TECHNOLOGY WE BOUGHT: ....

....

MAJOR MILESTONES: ....

» Births: ....

....

» Graduations: ....

....

» Marriages: ....

....

» Deaths: ....

....

favorite memory...

....

....

....

....

....

19 64

TOP NEWS STORIES: Warren Commission releases its report on JFK's assassination. Dr. Martin Luther King Jr. receives the Nobel Peace Prize. Nelson Mandela is sentenced to life in prison in South Africa. **GOVERNMENT:** Lyndon B. Johnson and Hubert Humphrey are elected president and vice president. Congress approves the Tonkin Gulf Resolution, escalating the Vietnam War. Southern senators filibuster for 75 days before the Civil Rights Act passes. Congress passes the Wilderness Act. President Johnson calls for a war on poverty. **MEMORABLE SONGS:** "Baby Love" by The Supremes • "Can't Buy Me Love" by The Beatles • "Chapel of Love" by The Dixie Cups • "I Feel Fine" by The Beatles • "A Hard Day's Night" by The Beatles • "The House of the Rising Sun" by The Animals • "I Get Around" by The Beach Boys • "I Want to Hold Your Hand" by The Beatles • "The Name Game" by Shirley Ellis • "Oh, Pretty Woman" by Roy Orbison • "She Loves You" by The Beatles **MEMORABLE MOVIES:** *Dr. Strangelove* • *A Fistful of Dollars* • *Mary Poppins* • *My Fair Lady* • *A Shot in the Dark* **SPORTS:** NFL Championship: Cleveland Browns • World Series: St. Louis Cardinals • Stanley Cup: Toronto Maple Leafs • World Figure Skating Championship: Sjoukje Dijkstra (Netherlands) and Manfred Schnelldorfer (Germany) • Wimbledon: Maria Bueno and Roy Emerson • U.S. Open: Maria Bueno and Roy Emerson • PGA Championship: Bobby Nichols • NASCAR Championship: Richard Petty **CELEBRITY BIRTHS:** Barry Bonds • Amy Brenneman • Sandra Bullock • Nicholas Cage • José Canseco • Courtney Cox • Russell Crowe • Matt Dillon • Chris Farley • Calista Flockhart • Vivica A. Fox • Melissa Gilbert • Teri Hatcher • Wynonna Judd • Rob Lowe • Michelle Obama • Ty Pennington • Keanu Reeves • David Spade **TRANSPORTATION:** Ford introduces the Mustang. Pontiac introduces the GTO. **TECHNOLOGY:** *Ranger VII* takes high-resolution pictures of the moon. **INVENTIONS:** 8-track audio recording cartridge • LCD displays **NEW PRODUCTS:** G.I. Joe doll • Creepy Crawlers **DISCOVERIES:** The Surgeon General links cigarette smoking with cancer. **FADS:** The monkey, chicken, watusi, and frug are popular dances. Beatlemania makes long hair fashionable for men.

CULTURE: The Beatles appear on *The Ed Sullivan Show*. Popular TV shows are *The Addams Family*, *Bewitched*, *Gilligan's Island*, *The Man from U.N.C.L.E*, and *Underdog*. *Funny Girl* and *Hello, Dolly!* are popular theater shows. ABC airs *Peyton Place*, the first prime-time soap opera. Head Start is established.

our 1 2 3

favorites

$

MILK
$1.06/gallon

GAS
$0.30/gallon

NEW HOME
$20,500

AVERAGE INCOME
$7,336/year

MINIMUM WAGE
$1.25/hour

FAMILY Milestones

WHERE WE LIVED: ....

....

....

JOBS WE WORKED OR YEAR IN SCHOOL: ....

....

....

CARS WE DROVE: ....

....

PEOPLE WE LOVED: ....

....

SONGS WE LOVED: ....

....

MOVIES WE LOVED: ....

....

TRIPS WE TOOK: ....

....

TECHNOLOGY WE BOUGHT: ....

....

MAJOR MILESTONES: ....

» Births: ....

....

» Graduations: ....

....

» Marriages: ....

....

» Deaths: ....

....

favorite memory...

....

....

....

....

....

19 65

TOP NEWS STORIES: Operation Rolling Thunder escalates the Vietnam War as B-52s selectively bomb North Vietnam. Antiwar protests break out; men burn draft cards. State police attack civil rights demonstrators in Selma, Alabama. Malcolm X is assassinated. Power blackout disrupts the Northeast. **GOVERNMENT:** President Johnson outlines his "Great Society" program. Congress passes the Voting Rights Act. Medicare is established. **MEMORABLE SONGS:** "Downtown" by Petula Clark • "Help!" by The Beatles • "Help Me, Rhonda" by The Beach Boys • "(I Can't Get No) Satisfaction" by The Rolling Stones • "I Can't Help Myself (Sugar Pie, Honey Bunch)" by The Four Tops • "I Got You Babe" by Sonny and Cher • "Mr. Tambourine Man" by The Byrds • "Stop! In the Name of Love" by The Supremes • "Ticket to Ride" by The Beatles • "Unchained Melody" by The Righteous Brothers • "Yesterday" by The Beatles • "You've Lost That Lovin' Feelin'" by The Righteous Brothers **MEMORABLE MOVIES:** *Doctor Zhivago* • *For a Few More Dollars* • *The Pawnbroker* • *The Sound of Music* **SPORTS:** NFL Championship: Green Bay Packers • World Series: Los Angeles Dodgers • Stanley Cup: Montreal Canadiens • NBA Championship: Boston Celtics • World Figure Skating Championship: Petra Burka (Canada) and Alain Calmat (France) • Wimbledon: Margaret Court and Roy Emeron • U.S. Open: Margaret Court and Manuel Santana • PGA Championship: Dave Marr • NASCAR Championship: Ned Jarrett **CELEBRITY BIRTHS:** Kristin Davis • Robert Downey Jr. • Dr. Dre • Horace Grant • Elizabeth Hurley • Kevin James • Diane Lane • Martin Lawrence • Reggie Miller • Sarah Jessica Parker • Luke Perry • Scottie Pippen • David Robinson • Chris Rock • Charlie Sheen • Brooke Shields • Shania Twain **TRANSPORTATION:** United Airlines orders 66 jetliners from Boeing with options for 39 more, the largest commercial airline order to date. Oldsmobile Tornado brings front-wheel-drive to the United States. **TECHNOLOGY:** *Early Bird*, the first commercial communications satellite, launches. **INVENTIONS:** AstroTurf • snowboard **NEW PRODUCTS:** Operation game • Barrel of Monkeys game **DISCOVERIES:** The first U.S. spacewalk. Scientists verify the cosmic background radiation predicted by the "Big Bang" Theory. **CULTURE:** Warning of health hazards is required on cigarette packs. *Days of Our Lives* TV soap opera debuts. Popular TV shows are *Get Smart*, *Green Acres*, *Hogan's Heroes*, and *I Dream of Jeannie*.

FADS: Mary Quaint introduces the miniskirt.
The "afro" becomes popular with young African-Americans.
Body painting and macrobiotic foods have followers.
"Flower Power" movement begins.

our

1

2

3

favorites

$

MILK
$1.05/gallon

GAS
$0.31/gallon

NEW HOME
$21,500

AVERAGE INCOME
$7,704/year

MINIMUM WAGE
$1.25/hour

FAMILY
Milestones

WHERE WE LIVED: ....

....

....

JOBS WE WORKED OR YEAR IN SCHOOL: ....

....

....

CARS WE DROVE: ....

....

PEOPLE WE LOVED: ....

....

SONGS WE LOVED: ....

....

MOVIES WE LOVED: ....

....

TRIPS WE TOOK: ....

....

TECHNOLOGY WE BOUGHT: ....

....

MAJOR MILESTONES: ....

» Births: ....

....

» Graduations: ....

....

» Marriages: ....

....

» Deaths: ....

....

favorite memory

....

....

....

....

19**66**

TOP NEWS STORIES: Four H-bombs fall from a B-52 over Spain. Richard Speck murders 8 student nurses in Chicago. Charles Whitman shoots 12 people at the University of Texas at Austin. **GOVERNMENT:** U.S. Supreme Court issues the Miranda Ruling. **MEMORABLE SONGS:** "Cherish" by The Association • "Good Vibrations" by The Beach Boys • "I Got You (I Feel Good)" by James Brown • "I'm a Believer" by The Monkees • "Monday, Monday" by The Mamas and the Papas • "Paperback Writer" by The Beatles • "The Sound of Silence" by Simon and Garfunkel • "Strangers in the Night" by Frank Sinatra • "Summer in the City" by Lovin' Spoonful • "These Boots Are Made for Walkin'" by Nancy Sinatra • "You Can't Hurry Love" by The Supremes **MEMORABLE MOVIES:** *Batman* • *Fantastic Voyage* • *The Good, the Bad, and the Ugly* • *Who's Afraid of Virginia Woolf?* **SPORTS:** NFL Championship: Green Bay Packers • World Series: Baltimore Orioles • Stanley Cup: Montreal Canadiens • NBA Championship: Boston Celtics • World Cup: England • NASCAR Championship: David Pearson • Wimbledon: Billie Jean King and Manuel Santana • U.S. Open: Maria Bueno and Fred Stolle • World Figure Skating Championship: Peggy Fleming (United States) and Emmerich Dánzer (Austria) • PGA Championship: Al Geiberger **CELEBRITY BIRTHS:** Troy Aikman • Stephen Baldwin • Justine Bateman • Halle Berry • Dean Cain • Deana Carter • Cindy Crawford • John Cusack • Patrick Dempsey • Salma Hayek • Janet Jackson • Julianna Margulies • Cynthia Nixon • Adam Sandler • David Schwimmer • Kiefer Sutherland **TRANSPORTATION:** The Motor Vehicle Safety Act passes. Dodge introduces the Charger. **TECHNOLOGY:** Soviet Union launches *Luna 10*, the first space probe to enter orbit around the moon. *Gemini 10* launches.

INVENTIONS: Dynamic random access memory (RAM)

NEW PRODUCTS: Taster's Choice instant coffee • Bac-Os • Twister game **DISCOVERIES:** Insulin is first synthesized in China. MIT biochemist Har Khorana finishes deciphering the DNA code. **FADS:** "Acid rock" dance halls have light shows accompanying acid rock music. The German Iron Cross becomes a short-term fad with the beach set. **CULTURE:** The Black Panther Party organizes. Stokely Carmichael promotes the Black Power movement. Activists found the National Organization for Women. Catholics are allowed to eat meat on Fridays except during Lent. The first endangered species list is issued. Popular TV shows are *The Avengers*, *Batman*, *Family Affair*, *The Monkees*, and *Star Trek*. John Lennon meets Yoko Ono.

our

1

2

3

favorites

$

MILK
$1.11/gallon

GAS
$0.32/gallon

NEW HOME
$23,300

AVERAGE INCOME
$8,395/year

MINIMUM WAGE
$1.25/hour

FAMILY
Milestones

WHERE WE LIVED: ....

....

....

JOBS WE WORKED OR YEAR IN SCHOOL: ....

....

....

CARS WE DROVE: ....

....

PEOPLE WE LOVED: ....

....

SONGS WE LOVED: ....

....

MOVIES WE LOVED: ....

....

TRIPS WE TOOK: ....

....

TECHNOLOGY WE BOUGHT: ....

....

MAJOR MILESTONES: ....

» Births: ....

....

» Graduations: ....

....

» Marriages: ....

....

» Deaths: ....

....

favorite memory...

....

....

....

....

....

....

19**67**

TOP NEWS STORIES: 474,000 U.S. troops are in Vietnam; 700,000 antiwar protesters march in New York City. Three astronauts die in the *Apollo I* fire. CIA illegally begins "Operation Chaos" to spy on antiwar activities and the "Stop the Draft" movement. **GOVERNMENT:** Tennessee's "Monkey Law" is repealed. Thurgood Marshall becomes first African-American on the Supreme Court.

MEMORABLE SONGS: "Daydream Believer" by The Monkees • "Happy Together" by The Turtles • "Hello Goodbye" by The Beatles • "Ode to Billie Joe" by Bobbie Gentry • "The Letter" by the Box Tops • "Light My Fire" by The Doors • "Somebody to Love" by Jefferson Airplane • "Strawberry Fields Forever" by The Beatles • "To Sir, With Love" by Lulu

---

MEMORABLE MOVIES: *Bonnie and Clyde* • *The Dirty Dozen* • *The Graduate* • *The Jungle Book* **SPORTS:** Super Bowl I: Green Bay Packers • World Series: St. Louis Cardinals • Stanley Cup: Toronto Maple Leafs • NBA Championship: Philadelphia 76ers • World Figure Skating Championship: Peggy Fleming (United States) and Emmerich Dánzer (Austria) • Wimbledon: Billie Jean King and John Newcombe • U.S. Open: Billie Jean King and John Newcombe • PGA Championship: Don January • NASCAR Championship: Richard Petty **CELEBRITY BIRTHS:** Pamela Anderson • Toni Braxton • Kurt Cobain • Harry Connick Jr. • Anderson Cooper • Vin Diesel • Will Ferrell • Jamie Foxx • Sophie B. Hawkins • Faith Hill • R. Kelly • Nicole Kidman • Matt LeBlanc • Dave Matthews • Tim McGraw • Julia Roberts • Anna Nicole Smith • Mira Sorvino **TRANSPORTATION:** Chevrolet introduces the Camaro. **TECHNOLOGY:** First successful human heart transplant is performed. Multiple Independently Targetable Re-entry Vehicle (MIRV), which allows one missile to carry several nuclear warheads, is developed. The atomic second becomes the time standard. **INVENTIONS:** Electronic handheld calculator **NEW PRODUCTS:** Amana's household microwave oven • *Rolling Stone* magazine **DISCOVERIES:** The first coronary bypass operation is performed. Biologically active DNA is synthesized. Pulsars are discovered. **FADS:** Psychedelic posters and "Head Shops" appear. Granny glasses, Nehru jackets, and antiwar buttons make the scene. **CULTURE:** Dr. Martin Luther King Jr. encourages draft evasion. Muhammad Ali refuses induction into the armed forces. Popular TV shows include *The Carol Burnett Show*, *Ironside*, and *The Smothers Brothers Comedy Hour*.

our

1

2

3

favorites

$

MILK
$1.15/gallon

GAS
$0.33/gallon

NEW HOME
$24,600

AVERAGE INCOME
$8,801/year

MINIMUM WAGE
$1.40/hour

FAMILY Milestones

WHERE WE LIVED: ....

....

....

JOBS WE WORKED OR YEAR IN SCHOOL: ....

....

....

CARS WE DROVE: ....

....

PEOPLE WE LOVED: ....

....

SONGS WE LOVED: ....

....

MOVIES WE LOVED: ....

....

TRIPS WE TOOK: ....

....

TECHNOLOGY WE BOUGHT: ....

....

MAJOR MILESTONES: ....

» Births: ....

....

» Graduations: ....

....

» Marriages: ....

....

» Deaths: ....

favorite memory

....

....

....

....

....

19**68**

TOP NEWS STORY: Robert F. Kennedy and Dr. Martin Luther King Jr. are assassinated. Riots occur in 125 cities following King's assassination. Chicago police beat demonstrators at the Democratic National Convention. The Vietcong launches the Tet Offensive.

GOVERNMENT: Richard Nixon and Spiro Agnew are elected president and vice president. **MEMORABLE SONGS:** "Hey Jude" by The Beatles • "I Heard It Through the Grapevine" by Marvin Gaye • "Love Child" by Diana Ross and The Supremes • "Mrs. Robinson" by Simon and Garfunkel • "People Got to Be Free" by The Rascals • "(Sittin' On) the Dock of the Bay" by Otis Redding • "This Guy's In Love with You" by Herb Alpert • "Tighten Up" by Archie Bell and The Drells • "What a Wonderful World" by Louis Armstrong **MEMORABLE MOVIES:** *2001: A Space Odyssey* • *Bullitt* • *Planet of the Apes* • *Romeo and Juliet* • *Yellow Submarine* **SPORTS:** Super Bowl II: Green Bay Packers • World Series: Detroit Tigers • Stanley Cup: Montreal Canadiens • NBA Championship: Boston Celtics • World Figure Skating Championship: Peggy Fleming (United States) and Emmerich Dánzer (Astria) • Wimbledon: Billie Jean King and Rod Laver • U.S. Open: Virginia Wade and Arthur Ashe • PGA Championship: Julius Boros • NASCAR Championship: David Pearson **CELEBRITY BIRTHS:** Patricia Arquette • Celine Dion • Brendan Fraser • Cuba Gooding Jr. • Tony Hawk • Vanilla Ice • Hugh Jackman • Ashley Judd • LL Cool J • Sarah McLachlan • Debra Messing • Gary Payton • Lisa Marie Presley • Rachael Ray • Mary Lou Retton • Molly Ringwald • Barry Sanders • Will Smith • Sammy Sosa • Owen Wilson **TRANSPORTATION:** Toyota introduces the Corolla, which will become the best-selling car in the history of the automobile. **TECHNOLOGY:** Frank Borman, James Lovell, and William Anders are the first people to orbit the moon in the first successful flight of *Apollo 8*. **INVENTIONS:** Automatic teller machine • Amniocentesis **NEW PRODUCTS:** Hot Wheels • Jacuzzi whirlpool **DISCOVERIES:** Pulsars and enzymes that cut DNA strands at certain points are discovered. **FADS:** The "Mod" and "Hippie" looks are in. **CULTURE:** *Hawaii Five-O* debuts. Popular TV shows are *60 Minutes*, *Julia*, and *Rowan & Martin's Laugh-In*. Yale admits women. The G, M, R, and X movie rating system is introduced. The rock musical *Hair* opens on Broadway.

our

1

2

3

favorites

$

MILK
$1.21/gallon

GAS
$0.34/gallon

NEW HOME
$26,600

AVERAGE INCOME
$9,670/year

MINIMUM WAGE
$1.60/hour

FAMILY
Milestones

WHERE WE LIVED: ....

....

....

JOBS WE WORKED OR YEAR IN SCHOOL: ....

....

....

CARS WE DROVE: ....

....

PEOPLE WE LOVED: ....

....

SONGS WE LOVED: ....

....

MOVIES WE LOVED: ....

....

TRIPS WE TOOK: ....

....

TECHNOLOGY WE BOUGHT: ....

....

MAJOR MILESTONES:

» Births: ....

....

» Graduations: ....

....

» Marriages: ....

....

» Deaths: ....

....

favorite memory

....

....

....

....

1969

TOP NEWS STORIES: Neil Armstrong and Buzz Aldrin land on the moon. The trial of the "Chicago 8" begins. Black Panthers Fred Hampton and Mark Clark are killed during a Chicago police raid. Sharon Tate and companions are murdered by the Manson cult. Mary Jo Kopechne dies when the car driven by Edward Kennedy crashes off the Chappaquiddick Bridge. Category 5 Hurricane Camille hits Mississippi coast, killing 248 and causing $1.5 billion in damage. **GOVERNMENT:** U.S. Supreme Court rules that the First Amendment applies to public schools in Tinker v. Des Moines Independent Community School District. **MEMORABLE SONGS:** "Aquarius/Let the Sun Shine In" by The Fifth Dimension • "Crimson & Clover" by Tommy James and The Shondells • "Dizzy" by Tommy Roe • "Everyday People" by Sly and The Family Stone • "Get Back" by The Beatles • "Honky Tonk Women" by The Rolling Stones • "I Can't Get Next to You" by The Temptations • "In the Year 2525" by Zager and Evans • "Sugar, Sugar" by The Archies **MEMORABLE MOVIES:** *Butch Cassidy and the Sundance Kid* • *Easy Rider* • *True Grit* **SPORTS:** Super Bowl III: New York Jets • World Series: New York Mets • Stanley Cup: Montreal Canadiens • NBA Championship: Boston Celtics • World Figure Skating Championship: Gabrielle Seyfert (Germany) and Tim Wood (United States) • NASCAR Championship: David Pearson • PGA Championship: Raymond Floyd • Wimbledon: Ann Haydon and Rod Laver • U.S. Open: Margaret Court and Rod Laver **CELEBRITY BIRTHS:** Jennifer Aniston • Jack Black • Cate Blanchett • Brett Favre • Steffi Graf • Ken Griffey Jr. • Anne Heche • Nancy Kerrigan • Jennifer Lopez • Marilyn Manson • Matthew McConaughey • Matthew Perry • Tyler Perry • Ellen Pompeo • Christian Slater • Gwen Stefani • Renee Zellweger • Catherine Zeta-Jones **TRANSPORTATION:** Plymouth Roadrunner is the hit of the year. Boeing 747 debuts. **TECHNOLOGY:** The first in vitro fertilization of a human egg is performed. The first message is sent over ARPANET, the forerunner to the Internet.

INVENTIONS: Household smoke detector • VCR • microprocessor

NEW PRODUCTS: *Penthouse* magazine • Nerf ball • Toss Across game • Wizzer toy **FADS:** Tie-dyeing, pantsuits for women, and bell-bottom pants become fashionable. **CULTURE:** Millions of Americans protest the Vietnam War during Vietnam Moratorium Day. New York's Stonewall Inn riot launches a gay rights movement. FCC bans all cigarette advertising on TV and radio. 400,000 attend Woodstock Music and Art Fair. The first Gap stores open. The Beatles give their last public performance.

our

1

2

3

favorites

$

MILK
$1.26/gallon

GAS
$0.35/gallon

NEW HOME
$27,900

AVERAGE INCOME
$10,577/year

MINIMUM WAGE
$1.60/hour

FAMILY
Milestones

WHERE WE LIVED: ....

....

....

JOBS WE WORKED OR YEAR IN SCHOOL: ....

....

....

CARS WE DROVE: ....

....

PEOPLE WE LOVED: ....

....

SONGS WE LOVED: ....

....

MOVIES WE LOVED: ....

....

TRIPS WE TOOK: ....

....

TECHNOLOGY WE BOUGHT: ....

....

MAJOR MILESTONES: ....

» Births: ....

....

» Graduations: ....

....

» Marriages: ....

....

» Deaths: ....

....

favorite memory

....

....

....

....

....

1970

TOP NEWS STORIES: National Guardsmen kill four student protestors at Kent State University. Vietnam peace talks in Paris continue. *Apollo 13* returns safely to earth. **GOVERNMENT:** Wage and pay freezes are instituted. Water Quality and Clean Air Acts pass. President Nixon restores the sacred Blue Lake to Taos Pueblo.

CENSUS RESULTS: U.S. population reaches 203,302,031. More than 3.3 million immigrants entered the United States in the previous decade.

MEMORABLE SONGS: "Ain't No Mountain High Enough" by Diana Ross • "American Woman" by The Guess Who • "Bridge Over Troubled Water" by Simon and Garfunkel • "I'll Be There" by The Jackson Five • "I Think I Love You" by The Partridge Family • "Let It Be" by The Beatles • "My Sweet Lord" by George Harrison • "Raindrops Keep Fallin' On My Head" by B. J. Thomas • "War" by Edwin Starr • "We've Only Just Begun" by The Carpenters **MEMORABLE MOVIES:** *Airport* • *The AristoCats* • *Love Story* • *M*A*S*H* • *Tora! Tora! Tora!* **SPORTS:** Super Bowl IV: Kansas City Chiefs • World Series: Baltimore Orioles • Stanley Cup: Boston Bruins • NBA Championship: New York Knicks • World Cup: Brazil • Wimbledon: Margaret Court and John Newcombe • U.S. Open: Margaret Courtand and Ken Rosewall • World Figure Skating Championship: Gabrielle Seyfert (Germany) and Tim Wood (United States) • PGA Championship: Dave Stockton • NASCAR Championship: Bobby Isaac **CELEBRITY BIRTHS:** Andre Agassi • Julie Bowen • Mariah Carey • Matt Damon • Minnie Driver • Tina Fey • Deborah (Debbie) Gibson • Heather Graham • Queen Latifah • Phil Mickelson • Chris O'Donnell • Gabrielle Reece • Kelly Ripa • Uma Thurman • Vince Vaughn **TRANSPORTATION:** The Boeing 747 begins commercial service. First successful Japanese sports car—Datsun 240Z—is sold in America. **TECHNOLOGY:** Floppy disks are introduced to store computer data. The first synthetic gene is created. **INVENTIONS:** Digital wristwatches • animal cloning **NEW PRODUCTS:** Safety caps appear on drug and other product containers. Dawn Dolls introduced. **DISCOVERIES:** Linus Pauling endorses Vitamin C to treat colds. The first black hole is located. **FADS:** Girdles and bras lose favor with younger women. **CULTURE:** *All My Children* TV soap opera debuts. 20 million Americans observe April 21 as Earth Day. Popular TV shows include *Evening at the Pops*, *The Mary Tyler Moore Show*, *Monday Night Football*, and *The Partridge Family*.

our

1

2

3

favorites

$

MILK
$1.32/gallon

GAS
$0.36/gallon

NEW HOME
$26,600

AVERAGE INCOME
$11,106/year

MINIMUM WAGE
$1.60/hour

FAMILY
Milestones

WHERE WE LIVED: ....

....

....

JOBS WE WORKED OR YEAR IN SCHOOL: ......

....

....

CARS WE DROVE: ....

....

PEOPLE WE LOVED: ....

....

SONGS WE LOVED: ....

....

MOVIES WE LOVED: ....

....

TRIPS WE TOOK: ....

....

TECHNOLOGY WE BOUGHT: ....

....

MAJOR MILESTONES: ....

» Births: ....

....

» Graduations: ....

....

» Marriages: ....

....

» Deaths: ....

....

favorite memory

1971

TOP NEWS STORIES: Several thousand Vietnam veterans throw away their medals on the Capitol steps to protest the war. *The New York Times* publishes the "Pentagon Papers." **GOVERNMENT:** U.S. Supreme Court upholds busing of schoolchildren to achieve racial balance. Voting age changes to 18. President Nixon imposes freezes on rents, wages, and prices, and devalues the dollar. **MEMORABLE SONGS:** "Brown Sugar" by The Rolling Stones • "Family Affair" by Sly and the Family Stone • "Go Away Little Girl" by Donny Osmond • "Gypsies, Tramps and Thieves" by Cher • "How Can You Mend a Broken Heart" by the Bee Gees • "Imagine" by John Lennon • "It's Too Late" by Carole King • "Joy to the World" by Three Dog Night • "Maggie May" by Rod Stewart • "One Bad Apple" by The Osmonds • "Rose Garden" by Lynn Anderson **MEMORABLE MOVIES:** *Carnal Knowledge* • *Dirty Harry* • *King Lear* • *The Last Picture Show* • *Shaft* • *Summer of '42* **SPORTS:** Super Bowl V: Baltimore Colts • World Series: Pittsburgh Pirates • NBA Championship: Milwaukee Bucks • Stanley Cup: Montreal Canadiens • World Figure Skating Championship: Beatrix Schuba (Austria) and Ondrej Nepela (Czechoslovakia) • Wimbledon: Evonne Goolagong and John Newcombe • U.S. Open: Billie Jean King and Stan Smith • PGA Championship: Jack Nicklaus • NASCAR Championship: Richard Petty **CELEBRITY BIRTHS:** Christina Applegate • Mary J. Blige • Snoop Dogg • Shannen Doherty • Jenna Elfman • Sara Evans • Jeff Gordon • Tom Green • Alison Krauss • Jared Leto • Ewan McGregor • Denise Richards • Kid Rock • Winona Ryder • Pete Sampras • Jada Pinkett Smith • Picabo Street • Tony Stewart • Mark Wahlberg • Kurt Warner • Kimberly Williams-Paisley • Noah Wyle • Kristi Yamaguchi **TRANSPORTATION:** The Brotherhood of Locomotive Engineers lets railroads scrap the 100-miles-a-day rule. Amtrak takes over most U.S. passenger rail traffic. Plymouth Barracuda, Chevrolet Vega, and Fort Pinto are introduced. **TECHNOLOGY:** Intel introduces a microprocessor. *Mariner IX* takes pictures of Mars' surface.

INVENTIONS: E-mail and food processor

NEW PRODUCTS: Mastermind board game • Texas Instruments' pocket calculator **DISCOVERIES:** Cho Hao Li synthesizes the growth hormone somatotropin. **FADS:** Hot pants appear for one season. Young men and women custom patch their jeans. **CULTURE:** The first Rainbow Family gathering occurs. Andrew Lloyd Webber's *Jesus Christ Superstar* musical is on Broadway. *All Things Considered* debuts on the radio. Popular TV shows are *All in the Family*, *Columbo*, *Masterpiece Theater*, and *The Odd Couple*.

our
1
2
3
favorites

$

MILK
$1.32/gallon

GAS
$0.36/gallon

NEW HOME
$28,300

AVERAGE INCOME
$11,583/year

MINIMUM WAGE
$1.60/hour

FAMILY Milestones

WHERE WE LIVED: ....

....

....

JOBS WE WORKED OR YEAR IN SCHOOL:

....

....

CARS WE DROVE: ....

....

PEOPLE WE LOVED: ....

....

SONGS WE LOVED: ....

....

MOVIES WE LOVED: ....

....

TRIPS WE TOOK: ....

....

TECHNOLOGY WE BOUGHT: ....

....

MAJOR MILESTONES: ....

» Births: ....

....

» Graduations: ....

....

» Marriages: ....

....

» Deaths: ....

....

favorite memory...

....

....

....

....

....

1972

TOP NEWS STORIES: B-52s bomb Hanoi and Haiphong. Five burglars are arrested at Democratic Party Headquarters in the Watergate Hotel. Woodward and Bernstein of *The Washington Post* crack the Watergate affair. **GOVERNMENT:** Richard M. Nixon and Spiro Agnew are re-elected president and vice president. Nixon goes to China to establish political ties. The military draft ends, and the armed services become all-volunteer. Congress passes a Water Pollution Control Act. Title IX, mandating equality for women in education and athletics, passes. **MEMORABLE SONGS:** "Alone Again (Naturally)" by Gilbert O'Sullivan • "American Pie" by Don McLean • "The Candy Man" by Sammy Davis Jr. • "The First Time Ever I Saw Your Face" by Roberta Flack • "A Horse with No Name" by America • "I Can See Clearly Now" by Johnny Nash • "Lean On Me" by Bill Withers • "Me and Mrs. Jones" by Billy Paul • "Without You" by Harry Nilsson **MEMORABLE MOVIES:** *Cabaret* • *The Getaway* • *The Godfather* • *The Poseidon Adventure* • *Solaris* **SPORTS:** Super Bowl VI: Dallas Cowboys • World Series: Oakland Athletics • NBA Championship: Los Angeles Lakers • Stanley Cup: Boston Bruins • World Figure Skating Championship: Beatrix Schuba (Austria) and Ondrej Nepela (Czechoslovakia) • Wimbledon: Billie Jean King and Stan Smith • U.S. Open: Billie Jean King and Ilie Nastase • PGA Championship: Gary Player • NASCAR Championship: Richard Petty **CELEBRITY BIRTHS:** Ben Affleck • Drew Bledsoe • Cameron Diaz • Eminem • Jennifer Garner • Jennie Garth • Grant Hill • Wyclef Jean • Jude Law • Jenny McCarthy • Joey McIntyre • Alyssa Milano • Shaquille O'Neal • Brad Paisley • Gwyneth Paltrow • Amanda Peet • Rob Thomas • Chris Tucker **TRANSPORTATION:** Mercedes-Benz introduces the 350SL. **TECHNOLOGY:** Atari introduces the arcade version of the video game Pong. **INVENTIONS:** Prozac • video games • CT scan **NEW PRODUCTS:** *Ms.* magazine • Hacky Sack **DISCOVERIES:** Hexachlorophene is banned.

FADS: Acupuncture becomes popular.

CULTURE: Sally J. Priesand becomes the first woman rabbi in the United States. Federal Express and Nike are founded. Bobby Fischer beats Russian chess champion Boris Spassky. *The Price is Right* with Bob Barker debuts. Popular TV shows are *The Bob Newhart Show*, *Emergency!*, *Fat Albert and the Cosby Kids*, *Kung Fu*, *M*A*S*H*, *Maude*, *Sanford and Sons*, and *The Waltons*.

our 1 2 3 favorites

$

MILK
$1.33/gallon

GAS
$0.36/gallon

NEW HOME
$30,500

AVERAGE INCOME
$12,625/year

MINIMUM WAGE
$1.60/hour

FAMILY Milestones

WHERE WE LIVED: ....

....

....

JOBS WE WORKED OR YEAR IN SCHOOL: ....

....

....

CARS WE DROVE: ....

....

PEOPLE WE LOVED: ....

....

SONGS WE LOVED: ....

....

MOVIES WE LOVED: ....

....

TRIPS WE TOOK: ....

....

TECHNOLOGY WE BOUGHT: ....

....

MAJOR MILESTONES: ....

» Births: ....

....

» Graduations: ....

....

» Marriages: ....

....

» Deaths: ....

....

favorite memory...

....

....

....

....

....

1973

TOP NEWS STORIES: Direct U.S. ground troop involvement in Vietnam ends. U.S. Supreme Court decision in Roe v. Wade legalizes abortion. **GOVERNMENT:** Vice President Spiro Agnew resigns amid charges of income tax evasion. Gerald R. Ford is sworn in as a vice president. Senator Sam Ervin Jr. heads the committee to investigate Watergate. **MEMORABLE SONGS:** "Angie" by The Rolling Stones • "Bad, Bad Leroy Brown" by Jim Croce • "Crocodile Rock" by Elton John • "Killing Me Softly with His Song" by Roberta Flack • "Let's Get It On" by Marvin Gaye • "Midnight Train to Georgia" by Gladys Knight and the Pips • "My Love" by Paul McCartney and Wings • "Top of the World" by The Carpenters • "You're So Vain" by Carly Simon **MEMORABLE MOVIES:** *American Graffiti* • *The Exorcist* • *The Sting* **SPORTS:** Super Bowl VII: Miami Dolphins • World Series: Oakland Athletics • NBA Championship: New York Knicks • Stanley Cup: Montreal Canadiens • NASCAR Championship: Benny Parsons • Wimbledon: Billie Jean King and Jan Kodeš • U.S. Open: Margaret Court and John Newcombe • World Figure Skating Championship: Karen Magnussen (Canada) and Ondrej Nepela (Czechoslovakia) • PGA Championship: Jack Nicklaus **CELEBRITY BIRTHS:** Kate Beckinsale • Neve Campbell • Dave Chappelle • Brian Austin Green • Neil Patrick Harris • Oscar de la Hoya • Jason Kidd • Heidi Klum • Lisa Ling • Mario Lopez • Monica Seles • Tori Spelling **TRANSPORTATION:** Honda introduces the Civic.

TECHNOLOGY: The Skylab is launched. Nuclear Magnetic Resonance (NMR), the technology behind MRI scanning, is developed. Universal Product Code label is recommended by the grocery industry.

INVENTIONS: Genetic engineering **NEW PRODUCTS:** Cuisinart kitchen machine **DISCOVERIES:** Marijuana is used to treat glaucoma. **FADS:** Silk-screened T-shirts are accepted as casual wear. Southwestern Indian jewelry becomes a fashion statement. **CULTURE:** Farm labor represents 5 percent of the U.S. workforce. Homosexuality is no longer classified as a mental disorder. Chicago's Sears Tower becomes the world's tallest building at 1,455 feet. Popular TV shows include *Barnaby Jones*, *The Midnight Special*, and *The Six Million Dollar Man*.

our
1
2
3
favorites

$

MILK
$1.36/gallon

GAS
$0.39/gallon

NEW HOME
$35,500

AVERAGE INCOME
$13,622/year

MINIMUM WAGE
$1.60/hour

FAMILY Milestones

WHERE WE LIVED: ....

....

....

JOBS WE WORKED OR YEAR IN SCHOOL: ....

....

....

CARS WE DROVE: ....

....

PEOPLE WE LOVED: ....

....

SONGS WE LOVED: ....

....

MOVIES WE LOVED: ....

....

TRIPS WE TOOK: ....

....

TECHNOLOGY WE BOUGHT: ....

....

MAJOR MILESTONES:

» Births: ....

....

» Graduations: ....

....

» Marriages: ....

....

» Deaths: ....

....

favorite memory...

....

....

....

....

....

1974

TOP NEWS STORIES: House Judiciary Committee votes to impeach President Richard Nixon. Nixon resigns; Gerald R. Ford becomes the 38th president. Karen Silkwood dies in an auto crash on the road to a meeting with a reporter to expose nuclear power cover-ups. The Symbionese Liberation Army kidnaps Patricia Hearst. **GOVERNMENT:** President Ford pardons Nixon. Congress passes an election reform act and Freedom of Information Act. **MEMORABLE SONGS:** "Annie's Song" by John Denver • "I Shot the Sheriff" by Eric Clapton • "Kung Fu Fighting" by Carl Douglas • "The Loco-Motion" by Grand Funk Railroad • "Seasons in the Sun" by Terry Jacks • "The Streak" by Ray Stevens • "The Way We Were" by Barbra Streisand **MEMORABLE MOVIES:** *Benji* • *Blazing Saddles* • *Chinatown* • *The Texas Chainsaw Massacre* • *The Towering Inferno* • *Young Frankenstein* **SPORTS:** Super Bowl VIII: Miami Dolphins • World Series: Oakland Athletics • NBA Championship: Boston Celtics • Stanley Cup: Philadelphia Flyers • NASCAR Championship: Richard Petty • Wimbledon: Chris Evert and Jimmy Connors • U.S. Open: Billie Jean King and Jimmy Connors • World Figure Skating Championship: Christine Errath (Germany) and Jan Hoffman (Germany) • PGA Championship: Lee Trevino **CELEBRITY BIRTHS:** Amy Adams • Christian Bale • Victoria Beckham • Penelope Cruz • Leonardo DiCaprio • Dale Earnhardt Jr. • Seth Green • Alyson Hannigan • Derek Jeter • Alanis Morissette • Nelly • Jerry O'Connell • Ryan Phillippe • Joaquin Phoenix • Ryan Seacrest • Hilary Swank • Tiffani Thiessen • Robbie Williams **TRANSPORTATION:** A 55 mph highway speed limit law goes into effect. Motorists experience gasoline shortages. Porsche introduces the 911. **TECHNOLOGY:** Word processors come into use. **INVENTIONS:** Personal computer **NEW PRODUCTS:** *High Times* magazine • *People* magazine • Connect Four game • Rubik's Cube **DISCOVERIES:** The National Science Foundation recommends a ban on some genetic manipulation. **FADS:** The string bikini debuts. "Streaking" has a brief exposure on college campuses.

CULTURE: *Little House on the Prairie* debuts on TV. The Heimlich Maneuver is popularized. The ban on ownership of gold is lifted. Money markets become available to small investors. Popular TV shows are *Chico and the Man*, *Happy Days*, *Police Woman*, *Rhoda*, and *The Rockford Files*.

our **1**
2
3 favorites

$

MILK
$1.39/gallon

GAS
$0.53/gallon

NEW HOME
$38,900

AVERAGE INCOME
$14,711/year

MINIMUM WAGE
$2/hour

FAMILY
Milestones

WHERE WE LIVED: ....

....

....

JOBS WE WORKED OR YEAR IN SCHOOL: ....

....

....

CARS WE DROVE: ....

....

PEOPLE WE LOVED: ....

....

SONGS WE LOVED: ....

....

MOVIES WE LOVED: ....

....

TRIPS WE TOOK: ....

....

TECHNOLOGY WE BOUGHT: ....

....

MAJOR MILESTONES: ....

» Births: ....

....

» Graduations: ....

....

» Marriages: ....

....

» Deaths: ....

....

favorite memory...

....

....

....

....

....

19**75**

TOP NEWS STORIES: Mayhem breaks out as the United States evacuates Saigon; the Vietnam War ends. President Gerald R. Ford escapes two assassination attempts. Rockefeller panel reveals the CIA and FBI kept secret files on American citizens. Jimmy Hoffa disappears. **GOVERNMENT:** President Ford signs the Metric Conversion Act. The Toxic Substances Control Act phases out PCBs. **MEMORABLE SONGS:** "Fame" by David Bowie • "Fox on the Run" by The Sweet • "Love Will Keep Us Together" by Captain and Tennille • "Mandy" by Barry Manilow • "My Eyes Adored You" by Frankie Valli • "Rhinestone Cowboy" by Glen Campbell • "Shining Star" by Earth, Wind, and Fire • "SOS" by ABBA • "That's the Way (I Like It)" by KC and the Sunshine Band

---

MEMORABLE MOVIES: *Jaws* • *The Man Who Would Be King* • *Monty Python and the Holy Grail* • *One Flew Over the Cuckoo's Nest* • *The Rocky Horror Picture Show*

SPORTS: Super Bowl IX: Pittsburgh Steelers • World Series: Cincinnati Reds • NBA Championship: Golden State Warriors • Stanley Cup: Philadelphia Flyers • NASCAR Championship: Richard Petty • World Figure Skating Championship: Dianne de Leeuw (Netherlands) and Sergey Nikolayevich Volkov (Soviet Union) • PGA Championship: Jack Nicklaus • Wimbledon: Billie Jean King and Arthur Ashe • U.S. Open: Chris Evert and Manuel Orantes **CELEBRITY BIRTHS:** Tiki Barber • Drew Barrymore • David Beckham • Mayim Bialik • Michael Bublé • Fergie • Sara Gilbert • Enrique Iglesias • Jimmie Johnson • Angelina Jolie • Eva Longoria • Tobey Maguire • Charlize Theron • Kate Winslet • Tiger Woods **TRANSPORTATION:** Volkswagen introduces the Rabbit economy car. **TECHNOLOGY:** Bill Gates and Paul Allen found Microsoft. Altair home computer kits allow consumers to build and program their own personal computer. **INVENTIONS:** Betamax videocassette recorder • VHS videocassette recorder **NEW PRODUCTS:** Lite beers • Holly Hobbie Oven **DISCOVERIES:** Lyme disease is identified in Lyme, Connecticut. **FADS:** The Hustle and Bump dances are popular in discos. Jumpsuits appear as casual wear. "Designer" jeans and gold neckchains become popular. **CULTURE:** Popular TV shows are *The Jeffersons*, *MacNeil/Lehrer News Hour*, and NBC's *Saturday Night Live*. Vietnamese "boat people" arrive in the United States.

our **1 2 3** favorites

$

MILK
$1.40/gallon

GAS
$0.57/gallon

NEW HOME
$42,600

AVERAGE INCOME
$15,546/year

MINIMUM WAGE
$2.10/hour

FAMILY Milestones

WHERE WE LIVED: ....

....

....

JOBS WE WORKED OR YEAR IN SCHOOL: ....

....

....

CARS WE DROVE: ....

....

PEOPLE WE LOVED: ....

....

SONGS WE LOVED: ....

....

MOVIES WE LOVED: ....

....

TRIPS WE TOOK: ....

....

TECHNOLOGY WE BOUGHT: ....

....

MAJOR MILESTONES:

» Births: ....

....

» Graduations: ....

....

» Marriages: ....

....

» Deaths: ....

....

favorite memory...

....

....

....

....

19**76**

TOP NEWS STORIES: United States celebrates its bicentennial. Nearly 2,000 students become involved in a racially charged riot at a high school in Pensacola, Florida.

GOVERNMENT: President Gerald R. Ford signs Federal Election Campaign Act. Jimmy Carter and Walter Mondale are elected president and vice president. The U.S. Supreme Court rules that capital punishment does not constitute cruel and unusual punishment. California enacts a right-to-die law. **MEMORABLE SONGS:** "Bohemian Rhapsody" by Queen • "Dancing Queen" by ABBA • "December, 1963 (Oh What a Night)" by the Four Seasons • "Disco Lady" by Johnnie Taylor • "Don't Go Breaking My Heart" by Elton John & Kiki Dee • "Tonight's the Night" by Rod Stewart **MEMORABLE MOVIES:** *All The President's Men* • *The Bad News Bears* • *Carrie* • *King Kong* • *Rocky* • *Taxi Driver* **SPORTS:** Super Bowl X: Pittsburgh Steelers • World Series: Cincinnati Reds • NBA Championship: Boston Celtics • Stanley Cup: Montreal Canadiens • NASCAR Championship: Cale Yarborough • Wimbledon: Chris Evert and Björn Borg • U.S. Open: Chris Evert and Jimmy Connors • World Figure Skating Championships: Dorothy Hamill (United States) and John Curry (Britain) • PGA Championship: Dave Stockton **CELEBRITY BIRTHS:** Candace Cameron • Colin Farrell • Kevin Garnett • Melissa Joan Hart • Peyton Manning • Piper Perabo • Freddie Prinze Jr. • Keri Russell • Alicia Silverstone • Reese Witherspoon **TRANSPORTATION:** Automobile mileage standards are mandated. Motor Trend names Dodge Aspen and Plymouth Volare as Cars of the Year. First commercial Concorde flight takes off. **TECHNOLOGY:** Fax machines become common. Genentech, Apple Computer, and WTBS in Atlanta are founded. The Steadicam is used for the first time in the *Rocky* movie. The first commercially developed supercomputer, the Cray-1, is released. **INVENTIONS:** Compact fluorescent lamp **NEW PRODUCTS:** Hello Kitty (in the US) • Stretch Armstrong action figure • Atari Video Computer System **DISCOVERIES:** The *Viking I* spacecraft lands on Mars. The first cases of Legionnaires' disease occur in Philadelphia. **FADS:** High-fiber foods become popular. Dorothy Hamill haircuts are popular. Farrah Fawcett posters are big sellers. EST (Erhard Seminars Training) is the latest form of self-realization. **CULTURE:** Rhodes Scholarships become available to women. Red Dye No. 2 is banned in foods. Popular TV shows are *The Bionic Woman*, *Charlie's Angels*, *Laverne & Shirley*, and *The Muppet Show*.

our

1

2

3

favorites

$

MILK
$1.42/gallon

GAS
$0.60/gallon

NEW HOME
$48,000

AVERAGE INCOME
$16,870/year

MINIMUM WAGE
$2.30/hour

FAMILY Milestones

WHERE WE LIVED: ....

....

....

JOBS WE WORKED OR YEAR IN SCHOOL:

....

....

CARS WE DROVE: ....

....

PEOPLE WE LOVED: ....

....

SONGS WE LOVED: ....

....

MOVIES WE LOVED: ....

....

TRIPS WE TOOK: ....

....

TECHNOLOGY WE BOUGHT: ....

....

MAJOR MILESTONES:

» Births: ....

....

» Graduations: ....

....

» Marriages: ....

....

» Deaths: ....

....

favorite memory

....

....

....

....

....

1977

TOP NEWS STORIES: Fluorocarbons are banned as aerosol propellants. President Jimmmy Carter pardons Vietnam War draft evaders. Leonard Peltier of the American Indian Movement is convicted of killing two FBI agents and sentenced to prison. **GOVERN-MENT:** President Carter makes human rights part of U.S. foreign policy. **MEMORABLE SONGS:** "Best of My Love" by The Emotions • "Evergreen (from A Star Is Born)" by Barbra Streisand • "Hotel California" by The Eagles • "How Deep is Your Love" by The Bee Gees • "I Feel Love" by Donna Summer • "Sir Duke" by Stevie Wonder • "You Light Up My Life" by Debby Boone **MEMORABLE MOVIES:** *Close Encounters of the Third Kind* • *Saturday Night Fever* • *Smokey and the Bandit* • *Star Wars Episode IV: A New Hope* • *The Turning Point*

SPORTS: Super Bowl XI: Oakland Raiders • World Series: New York Yankees • NBA Championship: Portland Trail Blazers • Stanley Cup: Montreal Canadiens • NASCAR Championship: Cale Yarborough • World Figure Skating Championship: Linda Fratianne (United States) and Vladimir Kovalev (Soviet Union) • Wimbledon: Virginia Wade and Björn Borg • U.S. Open: Chris Evert and Guillermo Vilas • PGA Championship: Lanny Wadkins

---

CELEBRITY BIRTHS: Oksana Baiul • Orlando Bloom • Vince Carter • Sarah Michelle Gellar • Maggie Gyllenhaal • Elisabeth Hasselbeck • Ludacris • Bode Miller • Brittany Murphy • Shakira • Liv Tyler • James Van Der Beek • Kanye West **TRANSPORTA-TION:** Gossamer Condor is the first human-powered plane. Chevrolet Caprice is Motor Trend's car of the year. **TECHNOLOGY:** Lasers are first used to initiate a fusion reaction. **INVENTIONS:** neutron bomb • MRI scanner **NEW PRODUCTS:** Apple II personal computer • consumer VHS recorders **DISCOVERIES:** Insulin is produced from genetically engineered bacteria. Balloon angioplasty is developed for opening clogged arteries. **FADS:** Billy Beer flops are popular. **CULTURE:** Lawyers are now allowed to advertise. Popular TV shows include *Chips*, *The Love Boat*, *Soap*, and *Three's Company*. *Roots*, a TV miniseries, breaks records for audience size.

our

1

2

3

favorites

$

MILK
$1.44/gallon

GAS
$0.64/gallon

NEW HOME
$54,200

AVERAGE INCOME
$18,264/year

MINIMUM WAGE
$2.30/hour

FAMILY Milestones

WHERE WE LIVED: ....

....

....

JOBS WE WORKED OR YEAR IN SCHOOL: ....

....

....

CARS WE DROVE: ....

....

PEOPLE WE LOVED: ....

....

SONGS WE LOVED: ....

....

MOVIES WE LOVED: ....

....

TRIPS WE TOOK: ....

....

TECHNOLOGY WE BOUGHT: ....

....

MAJOR MILESTONES:

» Births: ....

....

» Graduations: ....

....

» Marriages: ....

....

» Deaths: ....

....

favorite memory

....

....

....

....

....

1978

TOP NEWS STORY: Californians revolt against high taxes and approve Proposition 13. Jim Jones orders his cult followers to commit mass suicide at the People's Temple, Jonestown, Guyana. **GOVERNMENT:** The United States and Panama renew the Panama Canal treaties. The American Indian Religious Freedom Act passes.

MEMORABLE SONGS: "Boogie Oogie Oogie" by A Taste of Honey • "Le Freak" by Chic • "(Love Is) Thicker Than Water" by Andy Gibb • "Night Fever" by The Bee Gees • "Shadow Dancing" by Andy Gibb • "Stayin' Alive" by The Bee Gees • "Three Times a Lady" by The Commodores • "Wonderful Tonight" by Eric Clapton • "Y.M.C.A." by The Village People • "You're the One That I Want" by John Travolta and Olivia Newton-John

MEMORABLE MOVIES: *Animal House* • *The Deer Hunter* • *Grease* • *Halloween* • *Superman* **SPORTS:** Super Bowl XII: Dallas Cowboys • World Series: New York Yankees • NBA Championship: Washington Bullets • Stanley Cup: Montreal Canadiens • World Cup: Argentina • PGA Championship: Jack Mahaffey • NASCAR Championship: Cale Yarborough • Wimbledon: Martina Mavratilova and Björn Borg • U.S. Open: Chris Evert and Jimmy Connors • World Figure Skating Championship: Anett Pötzsch (Germany) and Charles Tickner (United States) **CELEBRITY BIRTHS:** Jason Biggs • Kobe Bryant • Topher Grace • Josh Hartnett • Katherine Heigl • Katie Holmes • Joshua Jackson • Ashton Kutcher • Michelle Rodriguez • Sage Rosenfels • Brian Urlacher • Usher **TRANSPORTA-TION:** The Double Eagle II is the first balloon to cross the Atlantic. The Airline Deregulation Act begins a phase-out of regulations. Chrysler introduces Dodge Omni, which steers the company from the brink of bankruptcy. **TECHNOLOGY:** Interferon is prematurely hailed as a cure for some cancers. **INVENTIONS:** In vitro fertilization **NEW PRODUCTS:** Hungry Hungry Hippos game **DISCOVERIES:** The first test-tube baby, Louise Brown, is born in London. **FADS:** Jogging outfits are fashionable for workouts. Genealogy becomes popular thanks to the TV miniseries *Roots*. **CULTURE:** Money market funds are a popular hedge against the high inflation rate. Gambling casinos open in Atlantic City, New Jersey. Jim Davis introduces the cartoon strip "Garfield." Popular TV shows are *20/20*, *Dallas*, *Fantasy Island*, *The Incredible Hulk*, *Mork & Mindy*, and *WKRP in Cincinnati*.

our 1 2 3 favorites

$

MILK
$1.44/gallon

GAS
$0.65/gallon

NEW HOME
$62,500

AVERAGE INCOME
$20,091/year

MINIMUM WAGE
$2.65/hour

FAMILY Milestones

WHERE WE LIVED: ....

....

....

JOBS WE WORKED OR YEAR IN SCHOOL: ....

....

....

CARS WE DROVE: ....

....

PEOPLE WE LOVED: ....

....

SONGS WE LOVED: ....

....

MOVIES WE LOVED: ....

....

TRIPS WE TOOK: ....

....

TECHNOLOGY WE BOUGHT: ....

....

MAJOR MILESTONES: ....

» Births: ....

....

» Graduations: ....

....

» Marriages: ....

....

» Deaths: ....

....

REMEMBER

favorite memory

....

....

....

....

....

....

19 79

TOP NEWS STORIES: Militants seize 52 hostages at the United States embassy in Iran Hostage Crisis. President Jimmy Carter engineers the Camp David Peace Accord between Israel and Egypt. A near meltdown occurs at Three Mile Island nuclear power plant. **GOVERNMENT:** Washington establishes diplomatic relations with Beijing. U.S. Supreme Court upholds affirmative action. The Department of Education achieves Cabinet-level status. **MEMORABLE SONGS:** "Bad Girls" by Donna Summer • "Hot Stuff" by Donna Summer • "I Will Survive" by Gloria Gaynor • "My Sharona" by The Knack • "Reunited" by Peaches and Herb • "Too Much Heaven" by The Bee Gees • "Video Killed the Radio Star" by The Buggles **MEMORABLE MOVIES:** *Alien* • *Apocalypse Now* • *Cheech and Chong's Up in Smoke* • *The Muppet Movie* • *Star Trek* **SPORTS:** Super Bowl XIII: Pittsburgh Steelers • World Series: Pittsburgh Pirates • NBA Championship: Seattle SuperSonics • Stanley Cup: Montreal Canadiens • NASCAR Championship: Richard Petty • World Figure Skating Championship: Linda Fratianne (United States) and Vladimir Kovalev (Soviet Union) • Wimbledon: Martina Mavratilova and Björn Borg U.S. Open: Tracy Austin and John McEnroe • PGA Championship: David Graham **CELEBRITY BIRTHS:** Aaliyah • Drew Brees • Dallas Clark • Claire Danes • Chris Daughtry • Jennifer Love Hewitt • Kate Hudson • Norah Jones • Heath Ledger • Rider Strong

---

TRANSPORTATION: Gasoline rationing goes into effect as oil embargo takes hold. A $1.5 billion federal loan guarantee plan is approved for Chrysler Corporation. Buick Riviera is Motor Trend's car of the year.

TECHNOLOGY: VisiCalc is the first spreadsheet program. **INVENTIONS:** personal stereo • polar fleece material **NEW PRODUCTS:** Reebok shoes • Sony Walkman • Sea Wees Dolls **DISCOVERIES:** The first case of AIDS is diagnosed. A black hole is discovered at the center of our galaxy. **FADS:** Designer jeans with straight "cigarette-legs" and painters' pants come into fashion. Star Wars action figures are popular. **CULTURE:** Nickelodon network launches. Sticker company Lisa Frank, Inc., is founded. *A Prairie Home Companion* and *Morning Edition* debut on NPR. Popular TV shows include *Dukes of Hazzard*, *Knots Landing*, and *Taxi*. ESPN begins broadcasting.

our 1 2 3 favorites

$

MILK
$1.50/gallon

GAS
$0.88/gallon

NEW HOME
$71,800

AVERAGE INCOME
$22,316/year

MINIMUM WAGE
$2.90/hour

FAMILY Milestones

WHERE WE LIVED: ....

....

....

JOBS WE WORKED OR YEAR IN SCHOOL:

....

....

CARS WE DROVE: ....

....

PEOPLE WE LOVED: ....

....

SONGS WE LOVED: ....

....

MOVIES WE LOVED: ....

....

TRIPS WE TOOK: ....

....

TECHNOLOGY WE BOUGHT: ....

....

MAJOR MILESTONES:

» Births: ....

....

» Graduations: ....

....

» Marriages: ....

....

» Deaths: ....

....

favorite memory

....

....

....

....

....

....

1980

TOP NEWS STORIES: A military mission to rescue U.S. hostages in Iran fails. John Lennon is shot to death. ABSCAM uncovers bribery of public officials. Love Canal, New York, is declared a disaster area due to toxic waste. Mount St. Helens erupts in Washington state. The Mariel Boatlift brings 125,000 Cuban refugees to the United States **GOVERNMENT:** Ronald Reagan and George H.W. Bush are elected president and vice president. The U.S. Supreme Court rules that genetically engineered life may be patented. The banking industry is deregulated.

CENSUS RESULTS: The U.S. population is 226,542,203. About 4.5 million immigrants entered the United States during the previous decade.

MEMORABLE SONGS: "Another Brick in the Wall" by Pink Floyd • "Another One Bites the Dust" by Queen • "Funkytown" by Lipps Inc. • "(Just Like) Starting Over" by John Lennon • "Lady" by Kenny Rogers • "Magic" by Olivia Newton-John • "Rock with You" by Michael Jackson • "Sailing" by Christopher Cross • "Upside Down" by Diana Ross • "Woman in Love" by Barbra Streisand **MEMORABLE MOVIES:** *Airplane!* • *The Blues Brothers* • *Caddyshack* • *The Empire Strikes Back* • *Friday the 13th* • *Nine to Five* • *Raging Bull* • *The Shining* **SPORTS:** Super Bowl XIV: Pittsburgh Steelers • World Series: Philadelphia Phillies • NBA Championship: Los Angeles Lakers • Stanley Cup: New York Islanders • World Figure Skating Championship: Anett Pötzsch (Germany) and Jan Hoffmann (Germany) • PGA Championship: Jack Nicklaus • NASCAR Championship: Dale Earnhardt • Wimbledon: Evonne Goolagong Cawley and Björn Borg • U.S. Open: Chris Evert and John McEnroe **CELEBRITY BIRTHS:** Christina Aguilera • Macaulay Culkin • Zooey Deschanel • Ryan Gosling • Jake Gyllenhaal • Isaac Hanson • Michelle Kwan • Matthew Lawrence • Christina Ricci • Tony Romo • Michelle Williams • Venus Williams **TRANSPORTATION:** Max and Kris Anderson cross North America on a nonstop balloon flight. Honda announces plans to build an auto plant in the United States. Ford F-Series truck becomes the best-selling vehicle on the planet.**TECHNOLOGY:** AT&T begins marketing 900 numbers. **INVENTIONS:** CDs **NEW PRODUCTS:** Cordless telephones • Big League Chew bubble gum **DISCOVERIES:** Toxic Shock Syndrome is reported. **FADS:** Strawberry Shortcake • Parachute pants **CULTURE:** Pregnant women are encouraged to avoid caffeine. CNN begins broadcasting. New TV shows include *Magnum, P.I.*, *Nightline*, and *Too Close for Comfort*. John Williams becomes conductor of the Boston Pops.

our 1 2 3 favorites

$

MILK
$1.60/gallon

GAS
$1.22/gallon

NEW HOME
$76,400

AVERAGE INCOME
$28,874/year

MINIMUM WAGE
$3.10/hour

FAMILY
Milestones

WHERE WE LIVED: ....

....

....

JOBS WE WORKED OR YEAR IN SCHOOL:

....

....

CARS WE DROVE: ....

....

PEOPLE WE LOVED: ....

....

SONGS WE LOVED: ....

....

MOVIES WE LOVED: ....

....

TRIPS WE TOOK: ....

....

TECHNOLOGY WE BOUGHT: ....

....

MAJOR MILESTONES: ....

» Births: ....

....

» Graduations: ....

....

» Marriages: ....

....

» Deaths: ....

....

favorite memory

....

....

....

....

....

1981

TOP NEWS STORY: The national debt surpasses $1 trillion. President Ronald Reagan survives an assassination attempt by John Hinckley Jr. The United States shoots down two Libyan jets. **GOVERNMENT:** Reagan fires 12,000 striking PATCO employees. Sandra Day O'Connor becomes first female U.S. Supreme Court Justice. **MEMORABLE SONGS:** "9 to 5" by Dolly Parton • "Bette Davis Eyes" by Kim Carnes • "Celebration" by Kool and the Gang • "Endless Love" by Diana Ross and Lionel Richie • "Jessie's Girl" by Rick Springfield • "Physical" by Olivia Newton-John • "Tainted Love" by Soft Cell **MEMORABLE MOVIES:** *An American Werewolf in London* • *Body Heat* • *Chariots of Fire* • *For Your Eyes Only* • *The Fox and the Hound* • *On Golden Pond* • *Raiders of the Lost Ark* • *Taps* **SPORTS:** Super Bowl XV: Oakland Raiders • World Series: Los Angeles Dodgers • NBA Championship: Boston Celtics • Stanley Cup: New York Islanders • NASCAR Championship: Darrell Waltrip • Wimbledon: Chris Evert and John McEnroe • U.S. Open: Tracy Austin and John McEnroe • World Figure Skating Championship: Denise Biellmann (Switzerland) and Scott Hamilton (United States) • PGA Championship: Larry Nelson **CELEBRITY BIRTHS:** Jessica Alba • Natasha Bedingfield • Hayden Christiansen • Roger Federer • Josh Groban • Paris Hilton • Jennifer Hudson • Alicia Keys • Beyoncé Knowles • Eli Manning • Chad Michael Murray • Natalie Portman • Britney Spears • Julia Stiles • Justin Timberlake • Jonathan Taylor Thomas • Ivanka Trump • Serena Williams • Elijah Wood **TRANSPORTATION:** The DeLorean DMC-12 is released. Ford introduces the Escort.

TECHNOLOGY: IBM introduces the PC. VCRs become a household item. Computer users can press Control-Alt-Delete to reboot.

INVENTIONS: MS-DOS **NEW PRODUCTS:** Post-it notes **DISCOVERIES:** Space shuttle *Columbia* makes her maiden voyage. The first U.S. test-tube baby is born. Scientists identify AIDS as a disease. **FADS:** MTV begins broadcasting. He-Man and the Masters of the Universe toys are popular.

CULTURE: Lady Diana Spencer marries Prince Charles. First Paintball game is played. Popular TV shows are *Dynasty*, *Falcon Crest*, *Hill Street Blues*, and *Simon & Simon*.

---

our **1** **2** **3** favorites

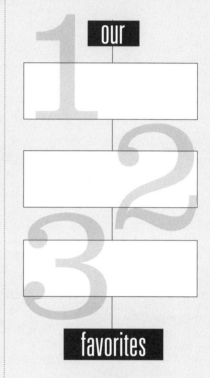

$

MILK
$1.69/gallon

GAS
$1.35/gallon

NEW HOME
$83,000

AVERAGE INCOME
$25,838/year

MINIMUM WAGE
$3.35/hour

FAMILY
Milestones

WHERE WE LIVED: ....

....

....

JOBS WE WORKED OR YEAR IN SCHOOL: ....

....

....

CARS WE DROVE: ....

....

PEOPLE WE LOVED: ....

....

SONGS WE LOVED: ....

....

MOVIES WE LOVED: ....

....

TRIPS WE TOOK: ....

....

TECHNOLOGY WE BOUGHT: ....

....

MAJOR MILESTONES: ....

» Births: ....

....

» Graduations: ....

....

» Marriages: ....

....

» Deaths: ....

....

favorite memory...

....

....

....

....

....

19**82**

TOP NEWS STORIES: Tylenol is recalled after seven die from capsules laced with cyanide. Grace Kelly, Princess of Monaco, dies in car crash. The world's largest oil rig, the Ocean Ranger, sinks in the north Atlantic. Severe recession begins in the United States. **GOVERNMENT:** President Ronald Reagan announces a "war on drugs." Reagan signs a bill that removes restraints on Savings and Loans. Ratification of Equal Rights Amendment fails. Vietnam Veterans Memorial is dedicated in Washington, DC. **MEMORABLE SONGS:** "Centerfold" by J. Geils Band • "Come On Eileen" by Dexy's Midnight Runners • "Eye of the Tiger" by Survivor • "Hard to Say I'm Sorry" by Chicago • "I Love Rock n' Roll" by Joan Jett and the Blackhearts • "Jack & Diane" by John Cougar Mellencamp • "Maneater" by Daryl Hall and John Oates • "Mickey" by Tony Basil • "Up Where We Belong" by Joe Cocker and Jennifer Warnes **MEMORABLE MOVIES:** *Blade Runner* • *Conan the Barbarian* • *E.T.: The Extra-Terrestrial* • *Ghandi* • *An Officer and a Gentleman* • *Poltergeist* • *Sophie's Choice* • *The Thing* • *Tootsie* • *TRON* **SPORTS:** Super Bowl XVI: San Francisco 49ers • World Series: St. Louis Cardinals • NBA Championship: Los Angeles Lakers • Stanley Cup: New York Islanders • World Cup: Italy • NASCAR Championship: Darrell Waltrip • Wimbledon: Martina Navratilova and Jimmy Connors • U.S. Open: Chris Evert and Jimmy Connors • PGA Championship: Raymond Floyd **CELEBRITY BIRTHS:** Jessica Biel • Kirsten Dunst • David Cook • Anne Hathaway • Adam Lambert • Kate Middleton • Andy Roddick • LeAnn Rimes • Kelly Clarkson • Tony Parker • Anna Paquin • Danica Patrick • Prince William of Wales **TRANSPORTATION:** Redesigned Pontiac Firebird goes on sale. Delorean Motor Company goes bankrupt. **TECHNOLOGY:** Barney Clark receives the first successful artificial heart. Liposuction introduced. Sun Microsystems and Adobe Systems are founded. Commodore announces release of Commodore 64 microcomputer. **INVENTIONS:** Camcorder **NEW PRODUCTS:** Cherry-flavored Coca-Cola • boxed milk • Gummy Bears • *USA Today* **DISCOVERIES:** A connection between Reyes' Syndrome in children and aspirin is established. FDA approves human insulin produced by bacteria.

FADS: Aerobic workout videos become popular.

CULTURE: TV soap *The Doctors* ends a 19-year run. *Cagney & Lacey*, *Cheers*, *Family Ties*, and *Knight Rider* TV shows debut. A computer scientist from Carnegie Mellon University suggests use of a smiley face (emoticon) as a way of expressing emotion in e-mail. Michael Jackson releases *Thriller*. Graceland opens to the public.

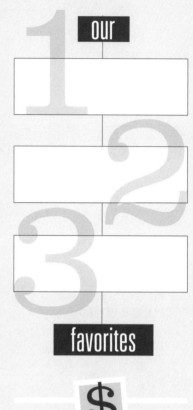

our

1

2

3

favorites

$

MILK
$1.79/gallon

GAS
$1.28/gallon

NEW HOME
$83,900

AVERAGE INCOME
$27,391/year

MINIMUM WAGE
$3.35/hour

FAMILY Milestones

WHERE WE LIVED: ....

....

....

JOBS WE WORKED OR YEAR IN SCHOOL:

....

....

CARS WE DROVE: ....

....

PEOPLE WE LOVED: ....

....

SONGS WE LOVED: ....

....

MOVIES WE LOVED: ....

....

TRIPS WE TOOK: ....

....

TECHNOLOGY WE BOUGHT:

....

MAJOR MILESTONES: ....

» Births: ....

....

» Graduations: ....

....

» Marriages: ....

....

» Deaths: ....

....

favorite memory

....

....

....

....

....

19**83**

TOP NEWS STORIES: Pope John Paul II signs new code that incorporates changes made by Second Vatican Council. United States invades Grenada. Space Shuttle *Challenger* makes successful maiden voyage with first U.S. woman astronaut, Sally Ride, on board. Soviet Union shoots down Korean Air Lines 747, killing all 269 on board. **GOVERNMENT:** Supreme Court reaffirms Roe v. Wade decision. President Ronald Reagan proposes a strategic defense initiative, dubbed "Star Wars." Martin Luther King Jr. Day becomes a national holiday. **MEMORABLE SONGS:** "Total Eclipse of the Heart" by Bonnie Tyler • "Billie Jean" by Michael Jackson • "All Night Long" by Lionel Richie • "Beat It" by Michael Jackson • "Flashdance" by Irene Cara • "Every Breath You Take" by The Police • "Say Say Say" by Paul McCartney and Michael Jackson • "Down Under" by Men at Work • "Baby, Come to Me" by Patti Austin and James Ingram **MEMORABLE MOVIES:** *Bad Boys* • *Cujo* • *Flashdance* • *The Outsiders* • *The Right Stuff* • *Risky Business* • *Scarface* • *Return of the Jedi* • *Terms of Endearment* • *Twilight Zone: The Movie* **SPORTS:** Super Bowl XVII: Washington Redskins • World Series: Baltimore Orioles • NBA Championship: Philadelphia 76ers • Stanley Cup: New York Islanders • NASCAR Championship: Bobby Allison • World Figure Skating Championship: Rosalynn Sumners (United States) and Scott Hamilton (United States) • PGA Championship: Hal Sutton • Wimbledon: Martina Navrátilová and John McEnroe • U.S. Open: Martina Navrátilová and Jimmy Connors **CELEBRITY BIRTHS:** Jessica Andrews • Kate Bosworth • Matt Leinhart • Jose Reyés • Aaron Rodgers • Martin St. Pierre • Taylor Hanson • Carrie Underwood • Vince Young **TRANSPORTATION:** Toyota introduces Camry to the American market. **TECHNOLOGY:** Microsoft releases Word. IBM releases the IBM PC XT, the successor to the original IBM PC.

INVENTIONS: Laptop computer

NEW PRODUCTS: CDs • NutraSweet • caffeine-free cola • Swatch watch **DISCOVERIES:** Barbara McClintock wins Nobel Prize in Physiology/Medicine for her discovery of mobile genes in the chromosomes of a plant that change the future generations of plants they produce. **FADS:** Breakdancing • suspenders • Cabbage Patch dolls • Monochichi • Rainbow Brite **CULTURE:** More than 125 million viewers tune in to last episode of *M*A*S*H*. *A Chorus Line* becomes the longest running show on Broadway. New TV shows include *Wheel of Fortune*, *The A-Team*, and *Night Court*. Crack cocaine is developed in the Bahamas and soon appears in the U.S.

our

1

2

3

favorites

$

MILK
$1.89/gallon

GAS
$1.23/gallon

NEW HOME
$89,800

AVERAGE INCOME
$28,638/year

MINIMUM WAGE
$3.35/hour

FAMILY
Milestones

WHERE WE LIVED: ....

....

....

JOBS WE WORKED OR YEAR IN SCHOOL:

....

....

CARS WE DROVE:

....

PEOPLE WE LOVED:

....

SONGS WE LOVED:

....

MOVIES WE LOVED:

....

TRIPS WE TOOK: ....

....

TECHNOLOGY WE BOUGHT: ....

....

MAJOR MILESTONES:

» Births:

....

» Graduations:

....

» Marriages:

....

» Deaths:

....

favorite memory

....

....

....

....

....

19 84

TOP NEWS STORIES: Reports of alleged child abuse at some day care centers cause hysteria. Twenty-two are killed in a shooting at a McDonald's in San Ysidro, California. Vanessa Williams is forced to give up her Miss America crown. Michael Jackson's hair catches fire while shooting a Pepsi commercial.

GOVERNMENT: Ronald Reagan is re-elected. Reagan cuts funding for international birth control programs. Geraldine Ferraro becomes first women to run for vice president. Due to de-regulation by the FCC, the first infomercials appear on TV. **MEMORABLE SONGS:** "Against All Odds" by Phil Collins • "Footloose" by Kenny Loggins • "Ghostbusters" by Ray Parker Jr. • "Jump" by Van Halen • "I Just Called to Say I Love You" by Stevie Wonder • "Karma Chameleon" by Culture Club • "Like a Virgin" by Madonna • "Time After Time" by Cyndi Lauper • "Wake Me Up Before You Go-Go" by Wham! • "What's Love Got to Do With It?" by Tina Turner **MEMORABLE MOVIES:** *Amadeus* • *Beverly Hills Cop* • *Footloose* • *Ghostbusters* • *Gremlins* • *The Karate Kid* • *Indiana Jones and the Temple of Doom* • *A Nightmare on Elm Street* • *Revenge of the Nerds* • *Sixteen Candles* • *Splash* • *The Terminator* **SPORTS:** Mary Lou Retton wins two gold, two silver and two bronze medals at the Olympics. Super Bowl XVIII: Los Angeles Raiders • World Series: Detroit Tigers • NBA Championship: Boston Celtics • Stanley Cup: Edmonton Oilers • NASCAR Championship: Terry Labonte • Wimbledon: Martina Navrátilová and John McEnroe • U.S. Open: Martina Navratilova and John McEnroe • World Figure Skating Championship: Scott Hamilton (United States) and Katarina Witt (East Germany) • PGA Championship: Lee Trevino **CELEBRITY BIRTHS:** Carmelo Anthony • Cheryl Burke • A. J. Foyt IV • LeBron James • Scarlett Johansson • Avril Lavigne • Mandy Moore • Kelly Osbourne • Katy Perry • Prince Harry of Wales • Brady Quinn • J. J. Redick • Ashlee Simpson • Lindsey Vonn **TRANSPORTATION:** Ford Bronco and Dodge Caravan minivan introduced. **TECHNOLOGY:** Apple introduces the "user friendly" Macintosh personal computer. William Gibson coins the term cyberspace. **INVENTIONS:** DNA fingerprinting • laserdisc storage **NEW PRODUCTS:** Rollerblades • GoBots **DISCOVERIES:** Scientists identify human immunodeficiency virus (HIV) as the cause of AIDS. Astronomers observe a distant solar systems being formed. Space shuttle *Discovery* is launched on its first mission. **FADS:** Stonewashed jeans • Trivial Pursuit board game • Teenage Mutant Ninja Turtles

our 1 2 3

favorites

$

MILK
$1.94/gallon

GAS
$1.20/gallon

NEW HOME
$97,600

AVERAGE INCOME
$31,052/year

MINIMUM WAGE
$3.35/hour

FAMILY Milestones

WHERE WE LIVED: ....

....

....

JOBS WE WORKED OR YEAR IN SCHOOL: ....

....

....

CARS WE DROVE: ....

....

PEOPLE WE LOVED: ....

....

SONGS WE LOVED: ....

....

MOVIES WE LOVED: ....

....

TRIPS WE TOOK: ....

....

TECHNOLOGY WE BOUGHT: ....

....

MAJOR MILESTONES: ....

» Births: ....

....

» Graduations: ....

....

» Marriages: ....

....

» Deaths: ....

....

favorite memory:

....

....

....

....

....

19**85**

TOP NEWS STORY: World oil prices collapse and banks heavily invested in oil production fail. Rock Hudson dies of AIDS. 8.0 magnitude earthquake hits Santiago, Chile. **GOVERN-MENT:** U.S. enacts budget-balancing bill. **MEMORABLE SONGS:** "Broken Wings" by Mr. Mister • "Can't Fight This Feeling" by REO Speedwagon • "I Want to Know What Love Is" by Foreigner • "Material Girl" by Madonna • "The Power of Love" by Huey Lewis & the News • "Say You, Say Me" by Lionel Richie • "Shout" by Tears for Fears • "We Are the World" by USA for Africa

MEMORABLE MOVIES: *Back to the Future • The Breakfast Club • Brewster's Millions • Cocoon • The Color Purple • The Goonies • Kiss of the Spider Woman • Out of Africa • Rocky IV • St. Elmo's Fire*

SPORTS: Pete Rose breaks Ty Cobb's all-time hit record. Super Bowl XIX: San Francisco 49ers • World Series: Kansas City Royals • NBA Championship: Los Angeles Lakers • Stanley Cup: Edmonton Oilers • NASCAR Championship: Darrell Waltrip • Wimbledon: Martina Navrátilová and Boris Becker • U.S. Open: Hana Mandlíková and Ivan Lendl • PGA Championship: Hubert Green • World Figure Skating Championship: Katarina Witt (East Germany) and Alexander Fadeev (Soviet Union) **CELEBRITY BIRTHS:** Kyle Busch • Haylie Duff • David Gallagher • Sarah Hughes • Keira Knightley • Frankie Muniz • Chris Paul • Adrian Peterson • Michael Phelps • Raven Symoné • Ashley Tisdale **TRANS-PORTATION:** Leaded gasoline banned. U.S. Route 66 is officially decommissioned. Nissan Maxima debuts. **TECHNOLOGY:** Minolta releases world's first autofocus single-lens reflex camera. FDA approves blood test for AIDS. DNA is first used in a criminal case. **INVENTIONS:** Scanning-tunneling microscope for visualizing images on an atomic scale **NEW PRODUCTS:** Pictionary board game • Nintendo Entertainment System • She-Ra: Princess of Power toys • Teddy Ruxpin • M.U.S.C.L.E. Man toys **DISCOVERIES:** Robert Ballard and team find the wreckage of the Titanic. British scientists report the opening of an enormous hole in Earth's ozone layer. **FADS:** Shoulder pads reappear in women's fashions. "Baby on Board" signs appear in car rear windows. Pound Puppies and The Care Bears become popular toys. **CULTURE:** Due to popular demand, Coca-Cola brings back its original formula, Classic Coke. Celebrities perform "Live Aid," a rock benefit for victims of famine in Africa. *The Golden Girls*, *Growing Pains*, and *MacGyver* TV shows air for first time. Montgomery Ward discontinues its mail-order catalog.

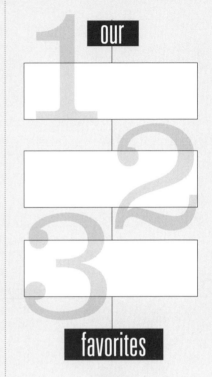

our

1

2

3

favorites

$

MILK
$1.98/gallon

GAS
$1.20/gallon

NEW HOME
$100,800

AVERAGE INCOME
$32,944/year

MINIMUM WAGE
$3.35/hour

FAMILY
Milestones

WHERE WE LIVED: ....

....

....

JOBS WE WORKED OR YEAR IN SCHOOL:

....

....

CARS WE DROVE: ....

....

PEOPLE WE LOVED: ....

....

SONGS WE LOVED: ....

....

MOVIES WE LOVED: ....

....

TRIPS WE TOOK: ....

....

TECHNOLOGY WE BOUGHT: ....

....

MAJOR MILESTONES: ....

» Births: ....

....

» Graduations: ....

....

» Marriages: ....

....

» Deaths: ....

....

favorite memory.

....

....

....

....

....

19**86**

TOP NEWS STORIES: The space shuttle *Challenger* explodes, killing all on board. Revelations of insider trading scandalize Wall Street. Major nuclear accident at Soviet Union's Chernobyl power station alarms world.

GOVERNMENT: U.S. Congress restructures the federal income tax system. The Iran-Contra Affair is exposed. U.S. Supreme Court upholds affirmative-action hiring quotas. U.S. Senate allows its debates to be televised on a trial basis. Goldwater-Nicholas Act authorizes major reorganization of the U.S. Department of Defense. **MEMORABLE SONGS:** "The Final Countdown" by Europe • "Greatest Love of All" by Whitney Houston • "Kiss" by Prince and the Revolution • "Kyrie" by Mr. Mister • "On My Own" by Patti LaBelle and Michael McDonald • "Papa Don't Preach" by Madonna • "Rock Me Amadeus" by Falco • "Stuck with You" by Huey Lews and the News • "Take My Breath Away" by Berlin • "That's What Friends Are For" by Dionne Warrick and Friends • "Walk Like an Egyptian" by The Bangles **MEMORABLE MOVIES:** *Aliens* • *An American Tail* • *Crocodile Dundee* • *Ferris Bueller's Day Off* • *Heat* • *Hoosiers* • *Labyrinth* • *The Money Pit* • *Platoon* • *Pretty in Pink* • *Three Amigos* • *Top Gun* **SPORTS:** Super Bowl XX: Chicago Bears • World Series: New York Mets • NBA Championship: Boston Celtics • World Cup: Argentina • Stanley Cup: Montreal Canadiens • NASCAR Championship: Dale Earnhardt • Wimbledon: Martina Navratilova and Boris Becker • U.S. Open: Martina Navratilova and Boris Becker • World Figure Skating Championship: Debi Thomas (United States) and Brian Boitano (United States) • PGA Championship: Bob Tway **CELEBRITY BIRTHS:** Mischa Barton • Jamie Bell • Amanda Bynes • Charlotte Church • Megan Fox • Lady Gaga • Shia LaBeouf • Lindsay Lohan • Heidi Montag • Mary-Kate and Ashley Olsen • Stacie Orrico • Candace Parker • Kellie Pickler • Brittany Snow • Shaun White **TRANSPORTATION:** *Voyager* completes the first nonstop circumnavigation of the Earth by air without refueling. Ford introduces Taurus, its best-selling model of all time. **TECHNOLOGY:** Soviet Union launches Mir space station. First e-mail list management software is developed. **NEW PRODUCTS:** Lazer Tag • Jenga game • Pop Secret microwave popcorn **DISCOVERIES:** *Voyager 2* probe passes Uranus and returns with images and data. **FADS:** Denim skirts **CULTURE:** Random drug testing is introduced to certain sensitive jobs. Study shows Americans watch more than seven hours of TV a day. Thousands of small farmers go bankrupt. FOX TV network begins operations.

our

1

2

3

favorites

$

MILK
$1.92/gallon

GAS
$0.93/gallon

NEW HOME
$111,900

AVERAGE INCOME
$34,924/year

MINIMUM WAGE
$3.35/hour

FAMILY
Milestones

WHERE WE LIVED: ....

....

....

JOBS WE WORKED OR YEAR IN SCHOOL:

....

....

CARS WE DROVE: ....

....

PEOPLE WE LOVED: ....

....

SONGS WE LOVED: ....

....

MOVIES WE LOVED: ....

....

TRIPS WE TOOK: ....

....

TECHNOLOGY WE BOUGHT: ....

....

MAJOR MILESTONES: ....

» Births: ....

....

» Graduations: ....

....

» Marriages: ....

....

» Deaths: ....

....

1987

TOP NEWS STORIES: The Dow Jones Industrial Average drops 508 points on Black Monday. "Baby Jessica" McClure falls down a well and is later rescued. America sends forces to the Persian Gulf to protect oil shipments. **GOVERNMENT:** Gary Hart's presidential campaign ends after allegations of sexual impropriety. U.S. Supreme Court rules that Rotary Clubs must admit women. Hearings on the Iran-Contra Affair and the Wedtech Scandal are held. Soviet premier Mikhail Gorbachev and President Ronald Reagan sign an arms reduction treaty. **POPULATION:** World population reaches 5 billion. **MEMORABLE SONGS:** "Alone" by Heart • "Faith" by George Michael • "I Wanna Dance With Somebody" by Whitney Houston • "La Bamba" by Los Lobos • "Livin' On a Prayer" by Bon Jovi • "Never Gonna Give You Up" by Rick Astley • "Nothing's Gonna Stop Us Now" by Starship • "Welcome to the Jungle" by Guns N' Roses • "With or Without You" by U2 **MEMORABLE MOVIES:** *3 Men and a Baby* • *Dirty Dancing* • *Fatal Attraction* • *Full Metal Jacket* • *Lethal Weapon* • *Moonstruck* • *The Princess Bride* • *RoboCop* • *Wall Street* • *The Untouchables* **SPORTS:** Super Bowl XXI: New York Giants • World Series: Minnesota Twins • NBA Championship: Los Angeles Lakers • Stanley Cup: Edmonton Oilers • NASCAR Championship: Dale Earnhardt • Wimbledon: Martina Navratilova and Pat Cash • U.S. Open: Martina Navratilova and Ivan Lendl • World Figure Skating Championship: Katarina Witt (Germany) and Brian Orser (Canada) • PGA Championship: Larry Nelson

---

CELEBRITY BIRTHS: Marco Andretti • Jay Bruce • Aaron Carter • Hilary Duff • Zac Efron • Jesse McCartney • Nicole "Snooki" Polizzi • Tim Tebow • Mara Wilson • Bow Wow

---

TRANSPORTATION: Richard Branson and Per Lindstrand make the first trans-Atlantic hot-air balloon flight. Chrysler acquires American Motors Corporation. First midsize pickup truck, the Dodge Dakota, is available. **TECHNOLOGY:** New Jersey Bell offers caller ID. Microsoft releases Windows 2.0. **INVENTIONS:** Laser vision correction • Perl programming language **NEW PRODUCTS:** Prozac • Snapple iced tea **DISCOVERIES:** Swiss and German scientists receive Nobel Prize in Physics discovering high-temperature superconductors. Supernova 1987A, the first "naked-eye" supernova since 1604, is observed. **FADS:** Popularity of board game Scruples leads to creation of computer versions of the game. **CULTURE:** Restrictions on smoking in public become commonplace. Aretha Franklin is first woman inducted into Rock and Roll Hall of Fame. *The Simpsons*, *Full House*, *Married … With Children* and *The Bold and the Beautiful* TV series debut.

our 1 2 3 **favorites**

$

MILK
$1.98/gallon

GAS
$0.96/gallon

NEW HOME
$127,200

AVERAGE INCOME
$36,884/year

MINIMUM WAGE
$3.35/hour

FAMILY Milestones

WHERE WE LIVED: ....

....

....

JOBS WE WORKED OR YEAR IN SCHOOL: ....

....

....

CARS WE DROVE: ....

....

PEOPLE WE LOVED: ....

....

SONGS WE LOVED: ....

....

MOVIES WE LOVED: ....

....

TRIPS WE TOOK: ....

....

TECHNOLOGY WE BOUGHT: ....

....

MAJOR MILESTONES: ....

» Births: ....

....

» Graduations: ....

....

» Marriages: ....

....

» Deaths: ....

....

favorite memory

....

....

....

....

1988

TOP NEWS STORIES: USS *Vincennes* shoots down an Iranian airbus in Persian Gulf after mistaking it for a jet fighter, killing 290. A terrorist bomb blows up a Pan Am Boeing 747 over Lockerbie, Scotland, killing 247. Iran-Iraq War ends.

GOVERNMENT: George H.W. Bush defeats Michael Dukakis in U.S. presidential race. United States formally apologizes for the World War II internment of Japanese-Americans. **MEMORABLE SONGS:** "Anything For You" by Gloria Estefan and the Miami Sound Machine • "Don't Worry Be Happy" by Bobby McFerrin • "Every Rose Has Its Thorn" by Poison • "Get Outta My Dreams, Get into My Car" by Billy Ocean • "A Groovy Kind of Love" by Phil Collins • "Heaven is a Place on Earth" by Belinda Carlisle • "Man in the Mirror" by Michael Jackson • "Roll With It" by Steve Winwood • "Simply Irresistible" by Robert Palmer • "Sweet Child O'Mine" by Guns N' Roses **MEMORABLE MOVIES:** *Beaches* • *Beetle Juice* • *Big* • *Big Business* • *Cocktail* • *Coming to America* • *Dirty Rotten Scoundrels* • *Die Hard* • *The Land Before Time* • *Rain Man* • *Who Framed Roger Rabbit?* • *Working Girl* **SPORTS:** Super Bowl XXII: Washington Redskins • World Series: Los Angeles Dodgers • NBA Championship: Los Angeles Lakers • Stanley Cup: Edmonton Oilers • NASCAR Championship: Bill Mears • World Figure Skating Championship: Katarina Witt (East Germany) and Brian Boitano (United States) • Wimbledon: Steffi Graf and Stegan Edberg • U.S. Open: Steffi Graf and Mats Wilander • PGA Championship: Jeff Sluman **CELEBRITY BIRTHS:** Kevin Durant • Julianne Hough • Vanessa Hudgens • Patrick Kane • Haley Joel Osment • Rihanna **TRANSPORTATION:** B-2 Stealth bomber is unveiled. Five-speed manual transmission and shift-on-the-fly transfer case are first used. **TECHNOLOGY:** Microsoft releases Windows 2.1. The first computer worm distributed via the Internet, the Morris Worm, is launched from MIT. Harvard scientists obtain patent for a genetically engineered mouse. **NEW PRODUCTS:** Teenage Mutant Ninja Turtles figures • Micro Machines • Super Mario Brothers 3 video game **DISCOVERIES:** NASA scientist James Hansen warns Congress of the dangers of global warming and the greenhouse effect. Studies determine that an aspirin a day reduces the risk of heart attack. **FADS:** CDs outsell vinyl records for the first time. Koosh Ball • Karaoke in the U.S. **CULTURE:** Ted Turner starts TNT network. 98 percent of U.S. households have at least one TV set. *China Beach*, *Murphy Brown*, *Roseanne*, and *The Wonder Years* TV shows begin.

our 1 2 3 favorites

$

MILK
$2/gallon

GAS
$0.96/gallon

NEW HOME
$138,300

AVERAGE INCOME
$38,608/year

MINIMUM WAGE
$3.35/hour

FAMILY Milestones

WHERE WE LIVED: ....

....

....

JOBS WE WORKED OR YEAR IN SCHOOL:

....

....

CARS WE DROVE: ....

....

PEOPLE WE LOVED: ....

....

SONGS WE LOVED: ....

....

MOVIES WE LOVED: ....

....

TRIPS WE TOOK: ....

....

TECHNOLOGY WE BOUGHT: ....

....

MAJOR MILESTONES: ....

» Births: ....

....

» Graduations: ....

....

» Marriages: ....

....

» Deaths: ....

....

favorite memory

1989

TOP NEWS STORY: Berlin Wall falls. Multibillion-dollar bailout of failed Savings and Loans begins. Hurricane Hugo devastates parts of the East Coast. Exxon Valdez spills 11 million gallons of oil into Alaska's Prince William Sound. Hundreds of Chinese civilians are killed during Tiananmen Square protests. Serial killer Ted Bundy is executed in Florida. Menendez brothers shoot their parents to death in the family's den. **GOVERNMENT:** President George H.W. Bush announces another "war on drugs." National Museum of the American Indian Act requires the return of Indian remains to their tribes. U.S. Supreme Court rules that burning the U.S. flag to protest government policies is a protected right. **MEMORABLE SONGS:** "Another Day in Paradise" by Phil Collins • "Blame it on the Rain" by Milli Vanilli • "Eternal Flame" by The Bangles • "Like a Prayer" by Madonna • "The Look" by Roxette • "Lost in Your Eyes" by Debbie Gibson • "Love Shack" by the B-52s • "Miss You Much" by Janet Jackson • "Right Here Waiting" by Richard Marx • "Straight Up" by Paul Abdul • "When I See You Smile" by Bad English • "We Didn't Start the Fire" by Billy Joel **MEMORABLE MOVIES:** *Batman* • *Born on the Fourth of July* • *Dead Poets Society* • *Driving Miss Daisy* • *Field of Dreams* • *Glory* • *Honey, I Shrunk the Kids* • *Indiana Jones and the Last Crusade* • *Look Who's Talking* • *The Little Mermaid* • *Steel Magnolias* • *When Harry Met Sally* **SPORTS:** Super Bowl XXIII: San Francisco 49ers • World Series: Oakland Athletics • NBA Championship: Detroit Pistons • Stanley Cup: Calgary Flames • NASCAR Championship: Rusty Wallace • Wimbledon: Steffi Graf and Boris Becker • U.S. Open: Steffi Graf and Boris Becker • PGA Championship: Payne Stewart • World Figure Skating: Midori Ito (Japan) and Kurt Browning (Canada) **CELEBRITY BIRTHS:** Ashley Benson • Chris Brown • Blake Griffin • Joe Jonas • Daniel Radcliffe • Jordin Sparks • Taylor Swift • Michelle Wie **TRANSPORTATION:** Top selling cars are Honda Accord, Ford Taurus, and Ford Escort. **TECHNOLOGY:** Robert Tappan Morris Jr., is first person prosecuted under 1986 Computer Fraud and Abuse Act for releasing a computer virus. McGill University researchers develop Archie, an archive of FTP sites—the first effort to index the Internet. **INVENTIONS:** World Wide Web **NEW PRODUCTS:** Polly Pocket toy • Nintendo Game Boy • Sega Genesis **DISCOVERIES:** *Voyager II* passes the planet Neptune and its moon Triton. The first McDonnell Douglas Delta II rocket launches the Navstar II-1 global positioning satellite.

FADS: Slap bracelets • "Dry" beers

CULTURE: *Baywatch*, *Family Matters*, *Life Goes On*, *Quantum Leap*, *Saved by the Bell*, and *Seinfeld* TV shows debut.

our
1
2
3
favorites

$

MILK
$2.15/gallon

GAS
$1.06/gallon

NEW HOME
$148,800

AVERAGE INCOME
$41,506/year

MINIMUM WAGE
$3.35/hour

FAMILY Milestones

WHERE WE LIVED: ....

....

....

JOBS WE WORKED OR YEAR IN SCHOOL: ....

....

....

CARS WE DROVE: ....

....

PEOPLE WE LOVED: ....

....

SONGS WE LOVED: ....

....

MOVIES WE LOVED: ....

....

TRIPS WE TOOK: ....

....

TECHNOLOGY WE BOUGHT: ....

....

MAJOR MILESTONES: ....

» Births: ....

....

» Graduations: ....

....

» Marriages: ....

....

» Deaths: ....

....

favorite memory...

....

....

....

....

....

19**90**

TOP NEWS STORIES: Iraq invades and annexes Kuwait, starting the Persian Gulf War. The United States deploys nearly 700,000 troops. Future South African president Nelson Mandela is released from prison after 27 years. East and West Germany reunite. **GOVERNMENT:** President George H.W. Bush signs the Americans with Disabilities Act.

CENSUS RESULTS: U.S. Population is 248,709,873. More than 7 million immigrants entered the United States in the previous decade. Courts no longer naturalize citizens.

MEMORABLE SONGS: "Friends in Low Places" by Garth Brooks • "Hold On" by Wilson Phillips • "How Am I Supposed to Live Without You" by Michael Bolton • "Ice Ice Baby" by Vanilla Ice • "It Must Have Been Love" by Roxette • "Janie's Got A Gun" by Aerosmith • "Nothing Compares 2 U" by Sinead O'Connor • "Opposites Attract" by Paula Abdul • "Pump Up The Jam" by Technotronics • "U Can't Touch This" by MC Hammer • "Vogue" by Madonna **MEMORABLE MOVIES:** *Arachnophobia* • *Dances with Wolves* • *Days of Thunder* • *Dick Tracy* • *Edward Scissorhands* • *Ghost* • *Goodfellas* • *Home Alone* • *Kindergarten Cop* • *Pretty Woman* • *Problem Child* • *Rocky V* • *Teenage Mutant Ninja Turtles* **SPORTS:** Super Bowl XXIV: San Francisco 49ers • World Series: Cincinnati Reds • NBA Championship: Detroit Pistons • Stanley Cup: Edmonton Oilers • World Cup: West Germany • NASCAR Championship: Dale Earnhardt • Wimbledon: Martina Navrátilová and Stegan Edberg • U.S. Open: Gabriela Sabatini and Pete Sampras • PGA Championship: Wayne Grady • World Figure Skating Championship: Jill Trenary (United States) and Kurt Browning (Canada) **CELEBRITY BIRTHS:** David Archuleta • Sean Kingston • Jonathan Lipnicki • Kristen Stewart • Emma Watson **TRANSPORTATION:** President Bush signs the Clean Air Act, mandating several pollution-reducing changes in the automobile and fuel industries. Mazda introduces the Miata roadster. Boeing 737 becomes the world's bestselling jetliner. **TECHNOLOGY:** Microsoft's Windows 3.0 • Hubble Space Telescope **NEW PRODUCTS:** Crystal Pepsi • *Entertainment Weekly* magazine • Super Soaker water gun • Adobe Photoshop **DISCOVERIES:** FDA approves Norplant contraceptive. Killer bees enter the U.S. National Center for Human Genome Research is created. Researchers grow human brain cells in laboratory. **FADS:** leggings and miniskirts • bungee jumping • New Kids on the Block • pet Vietnamese pot bellied pigs **CULTURE:** *America's Funniest Home Videos, Beverly Hills 90210, Fresh Prince of Bel-Air, In Living Color, Northern Exposure, Twin Peaks* and *Law & Order* debut on TV. Milli Vanilli admits to lip-synching. The MTV Unplugged series begins. Leonard Bernstein and Sammy Davis Jr. die.

our 1 2 3 favorites

$

MILK
$2.15/gallon

GAS
$1.22/gallon

NEW HOME
$149,800

AVERAGE INCOME
$42,652/year

MINIMUM WAGE
$3.80/hour

FAMILY
Milestones

WHERE WE LIVED: ....

....

....

JOBS WE WORKED OR YEAR IN SCHOOL: ....

....

....

CARS WE DROVE: ....

....

PEOPLE WE LOVED: ....

....

SONGS WE LOVED: ....

....

MOVIES WE LOVED: ....

....

TRIPS WE TOOK: ....

....

TECHNOLOGY WE BOUGHT: ....

....

MAJOR MILESTONES: ....

» Births: ....

....

» Graduations: ....

....

» Marriages: ....

....

» Deaths: ....

....

favorite memory...

....

....

....

....

19**91**

TOP NEWS STORIES: The Gulf War ends with Iraqi forces defeated and Kuwait liberated. The Soviet Union is dissolved. LAPD officers are videotaped beating Rodney King. Magic Johnson announces he has HIV. Paul Reubens (aka Pee Wee Herman) is arrested at a Florida movie theater for indecent exposure. The Tailhook Scandal reveals sexual harassment in the U.S. Navy. **GOVERNMENT:** Clarence Thomas is appointed to the U.S. Supreme Court amid controversy over sexual harassment charges by a former coworker. **MEMORABLE SONGS:** "Baby Baby" by Amy Grant • "Black or White" by Michael Jackson • "(Everything I Do) I Do It For You" by Bryan Adams • "Gonna Make You Sweat" by C&C Music Factory • "I Wanna Sex You Up" by Color Me Badd • "Losing My Religion" by R.E.M. • "More Than Words" by Extreme • "Right Here, Right Now" by Jesus Jones • "Smells Like Teen Spirit" by Nirvana • "Unbelievable" by EMF **MEMORABLE MOVIES:** *The Addams Family* • *Backdraft* • *Beauty and the Beast* • *City Slickers* • *Father of the Bride* • *Robin Hood: Prince of Thieves* • *Silence of the Lambs* • *Sleeping with the Enemy* • *Thelma & Louise* **SPORTS:** Super Bowl XXV: New York Giants • World Series: Minnesota Twins • NBA Championship: Chicago Bulls • Stanley Cup: Pittsburgh Penguins • World Cup: United States • NASCAR Championship: Dale Earnhardt • Wimbledon: Steffi Graf and Michael Stich • U.S. Open: Monica Seles and Stefan Edberg • World Figure Skating Championship: Kristi Yamaguchi (United States) and Kurt Browning (Canada) • PGA Championship: John Daly **CELEBRITY BIRTHS:** Emma Roberts • Erik Per Sullivan • Jamie Lynn Spears **TRANSPORTATION:** Ford Explorer, the best-selling midsize SUV of all time, debuts. Honda Accord, Ford Taurus and Toyota Camry are the best-selling cars of the year. First trans-Pacific hot-air balloon flight occurs. **TECHNOLOGY:** Texas Instruments produces the first optoelectrical integrated circuit (OEIC) chip. **INVENTIONS:** digital answering machine • Gopher Internet interface

---

NEW PRODUCTS: Super Nintendo Entertainment System

DISCOVERIES: Pierre-Gilles de Gennes wins Nobel Prize in Physics for discoveries about the ordering of molecules in substances ranging from "super" glue to an exotic form of liquid helium. **FADS:** Sports sandals **CULTURE:** *Blossom*, *Home Improvement*, *Rugrats* and *Step by Step* debut on TV. The Custer Battlefield National Monument is renamed the Little Bighorn Battlefield National Monument. Fox is the first network to permit condom advertising on TV. Nirvana releases *Nevermind* album.

our

1

2

3

favorites

$

MILK
$2.18/gallon

GAS
$1.20/gallon

NEW HOME
$147,200

AVERAGE INCOME
$43,237/year

MINIMUM WAGE
$4.25/hour

FAMILY
Milestones

WHERE WE LIVED: ....

....

....

JOBS WE WORKED OR YEAR IN SCHOOL: ....

....

....

CARS WE DROVE: ....

....

PEOPLE WE LOVED: ....

....

SONGS WE LOVED: ....

....

MOVIES WE LOVED: ....

....

TRIPS WE TOOK: ....

....

TECHNOLOGY WE BOUGHT: ....

....

MAJOR MILESTONES:

» Births: ....

....

» Graduations: ....

....

» Marriages: ....

....

» Deaths: ....

....

favorite memory

....

....

....

....

....

1992

TOP NEWS STORIES: Riots follow the acquittal of the four white Los Angeles Police Department officers in the beating of Rodney King. Four die in the shoot-out at Ruby Ridge, Idaho. U.S. troops deploy humanitarian mission to Somalia. Hurricane Andrew leaves 250,000 homeless in Florida.

GOVERNMENT: Bill Clinton and Al Gore are elected U.S. president and vice president. Pentagon authorizes a DNA identification system. U.S. lifts trade sanctions against China. FDA bans silicone breast implants. **MEMORABLE SONGS:** "Achy Breaky Heart" by Billy Rae Cyrus • "Baby Got Back" by Sir Mix-a-Lot • "Boot Scootin' Boogie" by Brooks & Dunn • "End of the Road" by Boyz II Men • "I'm Too Sexy" by Right Said Fred • "I Will Always Love You" by Whitney Houston • "Jump" by Kris Kross • "My Lovin' (You're Never Gonna Get It)" by En Vogue • "Save the Best for Last" by Vanessa Williams • "Tears in Heaven" by Eric Clapton • "Under the Bridge" by Red Hot Chili Peppers **MEMORABLE MOVIES:** *Aladdin* • *Basic Instinct* • *The Bodyguard* • *Dracula* • *A Few Good Men* • *Forever Young* • *The Last of the Mohicans* • *A League of Their Own* • *The Mighty Ducks* • *Sister Act* • *Under Siege* • *Wayne's World* **SPORTS:** Super Bowl XXVI: Washington Redskins • World Series: Toronto Blue Jays • NBA Championship: Chicago Bulls • Stanley Cup: Pittsburgh Penguins • NASCAR Championship: Alan Kulwicki • Wimbledon: Steffi Graf and Andre Agassi • U.S. Open: Monica Seles and Stefan Edberg • World Figure Skating Championship: Kristi Yamaguchi (United States) and Viktor Petrenko (Ukraine) • PGA Championship: Nick Price **CELEBRITY BIRTHS:** Miley Cyrus • Selena Gomez • Nick Jonas • Taylor Lautner • Cole and Dylan Sprouse **TRANSPORTATION:** The Dodge Viper goes on sale. **TECHNOLOGY:** WorldWideWeb browser • Kodak photo CDs **INVENTIONS:** Industrial lasers for peeling fruits and vegetables • text messaging **DISCOVERIES:** Genetically engineered plants produce biodegradable plastic. Comets are observed at the edge of the solar system in the Kuiper belt. The newest atomic clock loses only one second in 1.6 million years. **FADS:** Grunge music • *Barney and Friends* **CULTURE:** *Mad About You, Melrose Place, Picket Fences* and *The Real World* debut on TV. Johnny Carson hosts *The Tonight Show* for the last time, ending a 20-year run. Mall of America opens in Bloomington, Minn. CDs surpass cassette tapes as preferred medium for recorded music. Sinead O'Connor tears up a picture of the Pope on *Saturday Night Live*.

our

1

2

3

favorites

$

MILK
$2.14/gallon

GAS
$1.19/gallon

NEW HOME
$144,100

AVERAGE INCOME
$44,221/year

MINIMUM WAGE
$4.25/hour

FAMILY Milestones

WHERE WE LIVED: ....

....

....

JOBS WE WORKED OR YEAR IN SCHOOL: ....

....

....

CARS WE DROVE: ....

....

PEOPLE WE LOVED: ....

....

SONGS WE LOVED: ....

....

MOVIES WE LOVED: ....

....

TRIPS WE TOOK: ....

....

TECHNOLOGY WE BOUGHT: ....

....

MAJOR MILESTONES: ....

» Births: ....

....

» Graduations: ....

....

» Marriages: ....

....

» Deaths: ....

....

favorite memory

....

....

....

....

....

1993

TOP NEWS STORIES: World Trade Center bombing kills six people and injures 1,000. A 51-day stand-off at the Branch Davidian compound near Waco, Texas, ends with a fire that kills 76 people, including David Koresh. Flooding of Mississippi and Missouri rivers causes billions of dollars in damage. **GOVERNMENT:** $30 billion Strategic Defense Initiative ("Star Wars") is dissolved. Ruth Bader Ginsberg is appointed to U.S. Supreme Court. President Bill Clinton instates waiting period for handgun purchases and the military's "Don't ask, don't tell" policy on homosexuality. **MEMORABLE SONGS:** "Can't Help Falling in Love" by UB40 • "Dreamlover" by Mariah Carey • "Freak Me" by Silk • "I'd Do Anything for Love (But I Won't Do That)" by Meat Loaf • "I'm Gonna Be (500 Miles)" by The Proclaimers • "Informer" by Snow • "Nuthin' but a 'G' Thang"by Dr. Dre • "Runaway Train" by Soul Asylum • "That's the Way Love Goes" by Janet Jackson • "A Whole New World" by Peabo Bryce and Regina Belle • "Whoomp! (There It Is)" by Tag Team

MEMORABLE MOVIES: *Free Willy • The Fugitive • Groundhog Day • Indecent Proposal • In the Line of Fire • Jurassic Park • Mrs. Doubtfire • The Pelican Brief • Philadelphia • Schindler's List • Sleepless in Seattle*

SPORTS: Super Bowl XXVII: Dallas Cowboys • World Series: Toronto Blue Jays • NBA Championship: Chicago Bulls • Stanley Cup: Montreal Canadiens • NASCAR Championship: Dale Earnhardt • Wimbledon: Steffi Graf and Pete Sampras • U.S. Open: Steffi Graf and Pete Sampras • World Figure Skating Championship: Oksana Baiul (Ukraine) and Kurt Browning (Canada) • PGA Championship: Paul Azinger **CELEBRITY BIRTHS:** Miranda Cosgrove • Ali Lohan • Taylor Momsen **TECHNOLOGY:** Mosaic graphical browser • Global positioning system (GPS) technology • Pentium processor **DISCOVERIES:** The occupants of Biosphere 2 emerge from their structure after two years of containment. The first test of the Delta Clipper rocket is successful. Human embryos are successfully cloned. **FADS:** Country line dancing • Pogs **CULTURE:** Sears Roebuck discontinues its general merchandise catalog. Barbra Streisand performs her first live public concert in 20 years. *Boy Meets World, Dr. Quinn, Medicine Woman, Frasier, Lois & Clark: The New Adventures of Superman, Mighty Morphin Power Rangers, NYPD Blue, Walker, Texas Ranger* and *The X-Files* debut on TV. Audrey Hepburn and Dizzy Gillespie die.

our 1 2 3 favorites

$

MILK
$2.27/gallon

GAS
$1.17/gallon

NEW HOME
$147,700

AVERAGE INCOME
$47,221/year

MINIMUM WAGE
$4.25/hour

FAMILY Milestones

WHERE WE LIVED: ....

....

....

JOBS WE WORKED OR YEAR IN SCHOOL: ....

....

....

CARS WE DROVE: ....

....

PEOPLE WE LOVED: ....

....

SONGS WE LOVED: ....

....

MOVIES WE LOVED: ....

....

TRIPS WE TOOK: ....

....

TECHNOLOGY WE BOUGHT: ....

....

MAJOR MILESTONES: ....

» Births: ....

....

» Graduations: ....

....

» Marriages: ....

....

» Deaths: ....

....

favorite memory

....

....

....

....

....

19**94**

TOP NEWS STORIES: U.S. troops intervene in Haiti. Nelson Mandela becomes the first black president of South Africa. Aldrich Ames is convicted of spying for the Soviet Union. American Michael Fay is caned in Singapore. O.J. Simpson arrested after a nationally televised low-speed police chase. Susan Smith drowns her two sons. Olympic ice skater Nancy Kerrigan is clubbed in the knee. **GOVERNMENT:** Republicans win control of both houses of Congress for first time in 40 years. President Bill Clinton signs the assault weapons ban. **MEMORABLE SONGS:** "All For Love" by Bryan Adams, Rod Stewart and Sting • "Black Hole Sun" by Soundgarden • "Breathe Again" by Toni Braxton • "Bump n' Grind" by R. Kelly • "Can You Feel The Love Tonight" by Elton John • "I'll Make Love to You" by Boyz II Men • "I Swear" by All-4-One • "The Power of Love" by Celine Dion • "Return to Innocence" by Enigma • "The Sign" by Ace of Base • "Stay (I Missed You)" by Lisa Loeb • "Whatta Man" by Salt-N-Pepa featuring En Vogue • "Wild Night" by John Mellencamp and Meshell Ndegeocello • "XXX's and OOO's (An American Girl)" by Trisha Yearwood **MEMORABLE MOVIES:** *Ace Ventura: Pet Detective* • *Clear and Present Danger* • *Dumb and Dumber* • *The Flintstones* • *Forrest Gump* • *Interview with a Vampire* • *The Lion King* • *The Mask* • *Pulp Fiction* • *The Santa Clause* • *Shawshank Redemption* • *Speed* • *True Lies* **SPORTS:** Super Bowl XXVIII: Dallas Cowboys • NBA Championship: Houston Rockets • Stanley Cup: New York Rangers • World Cup: Brazil • PGA Championship: Nick Price • NASCAR Championship: Dale Earnhardt • World Figure Skating Championship: Yuka Sato (Japan) and Elvis Stojko (Canada) • Wimbledon: Conchita Martínez and Pete Sampras • U.S. Open: Arantxa Sánchez Vicario and Andre Agassi **CELEBRITY BIRTHS:** Justin Bieber • Dakota Fanning **TRANSPORTATION:** United Airlines employees become majority shareholders. First year for V10 engine and optional four-speed automatic, as well as standard driver-side airbag and optical four-wheel anti-lock braking system. **TECHNOLOGY:** New Intelink network allows spy agencies to access secret information from almost anywhere. First cyberbank opens. **DISCOVERIES:** Existence of planets beyond our solar system is confirmed.

CULTURE: *Babylon 5, Ellen, ER, Friends, Party of Five* and *Touched by an Angel* debut on TV. Jackie Kennedy Onassis dies. Nirvana singer Kurt Cobain commits suicide.

our

1

2

3

favorites

$

MILK
$2.29/gallon

GAS
$1.17/gallon

NEW HOME
$154,500

AVERAGE INCOME
$49,340/year

MINIMUM WAGE
$4.25/hour

FAMILY Milestones

WHERE WE LIVED: ....

....

....

JOBS WE WORKED OR YEAR IN SCHOOL: ....

....

....

CARS WE DROVE: ....

....

PEOPLE WE LOVED: ....

....

SONGS WE LOVED: ....

....

MOVIES WE LOVED: ....

....

TRIPS WE TOOK: ....

....

TECHNOLOGY WE BOUGHT: ....

....

MAJOR MILESTONES: ....

» Births: ....

....

» Graduations: ....

....

» Marriages: ....

....

» Deaths: ....

....

favorite memory...

....

....

....

....

....

19**95**

TOP NEWS STORIES: Car bomb explodes outside the federal building in Oklahoma City, killing 168. U.S. troops deployed as peacekeepers in the Balkans. O.J. Simpson is acquitted of the murders of Nicole Simpson and Ronald Goldman. Tejano singer Selena is killed by the former president of her fan club. Million Man March occurs in Washington, DC. Unabomber manifesto is published.

GOVERNMENT: Republican Sen. Bob Packwood resigns from the Senate amid sexual harassment charges. Former Secretary of Defense Robert McNamara calls the Vietnam War a grave mistake. **MEMORABLE SONGS**: "Another Night" by Real McCoy • "Boombastic" by Shaggy • "Fantasy" by Mariah Carey • "Hold My Hand" by Hootie and the Blowfish • "Gangsta's Paradise" by Coolio • "I'll Be There for You" by The Rembrandts • "Kiss From a Rose" by Seal • "On Bended Knee" by Boyz II Men • "Take a Bow" by Madonna • "This is How We Do It" by Montell Jordan • "Waterfalls" by TLC • "You Oughta Know" by Alanis Morisette **MEMORABLE MOVIES:** *Apollo 13* • *Braveheart* • *The Bridges of Madison County* • *Clueless* • *Dangerous Minds* • *GoldenEye* • *Mr. Holland's Opus* • *Pocahontas* • *Seven* • *Toy Story* • *Waterworld* **SPORTS:** Super Bowl XXIX: San Francisco 49ers • World Series: Atlanta Braves • NBA Championship: Houston Rockets • Stanley Cup: New Jersey Devils • NASCAR Championship: Jeff Gordon • Wimbledon: Steffi Graf and Pete Sampras • U.S. Open: Steffi Graf and Pete Sampras • World Figure Skating Championship: Chen Lu (China) and Elvis Stojko (Canada) • PGA Championship: Steve Elkington **TRANSPORTATION:** A solar-powered airplane attains an altitude of 15,400 meters. The federal government allows states to set their own speed limits on interstate highways. Steve Fossett makes first solo transpacific hot-air balloon flight. **TECHNOLOGY:** An electromagnetic gun detector is developed. Internet Explorer is introduced. Amazon.com launches. *Toy Story*, first computer-animated movie, is released. **INVENTIONS:** DVDs • JavaScript computer language • mouse scroll wheel **NEW PRODUCTS:** Windows 95 • Sega Saturn gaming system **DISCOVERIES:** Ian Wilmut and Keith Campbell create Dolly, the world's first cloned sheep. Space shuttle *Atlantis* docks with the Russian space station *Mir* **FADS:** Melatonin • Beanie Babies **CULTURE:** Rock and Roll Hall of Fame Museum opens in Cleveland. WB television network launches. Actor Christopher Reeve is paralyzed. Final "Calvin & Hobbes" comic strip is published.

our 1 2 3 favorites

$

MILK
$2.51/gallon

GAS
$1.21/gallon

NEW HOME
$158,700

AVERAGE INCOME
$51,353/year

MINIMUM WAGE
$4.25/hour

FAMILY
Milestones

WHERE WE LIVED: ....

....

....

JOBS WE WORKED OR YEAR IN SCHOOL: ....

....

....

CARS WE DROVE: ....

....

PEOPLE WE LOVED: ....

....

SONGS WE LOVED: ....

....

MOVIES WE LOVED: ....

....

TRIPS WE TOOK: ....

....

TECHNOLOGY WE BOUGHT: ....

....

MAJOR MILESTONES:

» Births: ....

....

» Graduations: ....

....

» Marriages: ....

....

» Deaths: ....

....

favorite memory

....

....

....

....

19**96**

TOP NEWS STORY: Bombing kills one and injures 111 at 1996 Summer Olympics in Atlanta. Unabomber Ted Kaczynski arrested. One of the worst blizzards in American history hits Eastern states, killing more than 150 people. U.S. launches Operation Desert Strike against Iraq during Kurdish Civil War. JonBenét Ramsey is murdered in the basement of her parents' home in Colorado. **GOVERNMENT:** President Bill Clinton signs welfare reform and Electronic Freedom of Information Act Amendments into law. Clinton defeats Bob Dole in presidential election **MEMORABLE SONGS:** "Always Be My Baby" by Mariah Carey • "Because You Loved Me" by Celine Dion • "C'mon n' Ride It (The Train)" by Quad City DJs • "Give Me One Reason" by Tracy Chapman • "I Love You Always Forever" by Donna Lewis • "Macarena" by Los Del Rio • "Tha Crossroads" by Bone Thugs-N-Harmony • "Wonderwall" by Oasis **MEMORABLE MOVIES:** *The English Patient* • *Happy Gilmore* • *Independence Day* • *Jerry Maguire* • *Mission: Impossible* • *The Nutty Professor* • *One Fine Day* • *Ransom* • *Romeo + Juliet* • *Scream* • *Twister* **SPORTS:** Super Bowl XXX: Dallas Cowboys • NBA Championship: Chicago Bulls • Stanley Cup: Colorado Avalanche • NASCAR Championship: Terry Labonte • Wimbledon: Steffi Graf and Richard Krajicek • U.S. Open: Steffi Graf and Pete Sampras • World Figure Skating Championship: Michelle Kwan (United States) and Todd Eldredge (United States) • PGA Championship: Mark Brooks **CELEBRITY BIRTHS:** Abigail Breslin **TRANSPORTATION:** DarkStar, an unmanned aerial vehicle designed and built by Boeing and Lockheed Martin, makes first flight. Mercedes-Benz first uses four-headlight front-end system. **TECHNOLOGY:** Motorola introduces Motorola StarTAC Wearable Cellular Telephone, the world's smallest and lightest mobile phone at the time. Chess computer "Deep Blue" defeats world chess champion Garry Kasparov. NASA launches Mars Global Surveyor. Steve Jobs' company NeXT is bought by Apple, the company he co-founded. WebTV is introduced. **NEW PRODUCTS:** Nintendo 64 • Pokémon toys • PalmPilot personal digital assistant • Olympic Gymnast Barbie doll **DISCOVERIES:** Dolly the sheep, the first mammal to be successfully closed from an adult cell, is born in Scotland. NASA announces the ALH 84011 meteorite, thought to originate from Mars, contains evidence of primitive lifeforms.

FADS: Tickle Me Elmo • microbrews • the Macarena dance

CULTURE: Prince Charles and Princess Diana officially divorce. O.J. Simpson civil trial begins. *The Daily Show*, *Judge Judy*, and the *Rosie O'Donnell Show* debut on TV.

our

1

2

3

favorites

$

MILK
$2.72/gallon

GAS
$1.60/gallon

NEW HOME
$166,400

AVERAGE INCOME
$53,676/year

MINIMUM WAGE
$4.75/hour

FAMILY Milestones

WHERE WE LIVED: ....

....

....

JOBS WE WORKED OR YEAR IN SCHOOL: ....

....

....

CARS WE DROVE: ....

....

PEOPLE WE LOVED: ....

....

SONGS WE LOVED: ....

....

MOVIES WE LOVED: ....

....

TRIPS WE TOOK: ....

....

TECHNOLOGY WE BOUGHT: ....

....

MAJOR MILESTONES: ....

» Births: ....

....

» Graduations: ....

....

» Marriages: ....

....

» Deaths: ....

....

favorite memory

....

....

....

....

....

19**97**

TOP NEWS STORIES: Hong Kong returns to Chinese rule. O.J. Simpson found liable in wrongful death civil lawsuit. Timothy J. McVeigh receives death sentence for Oklahoma City bombing. Princess Diana dies in a car crash. Heaven's Gate cult members commit suicide. **GOVERNMENT:** U.S. Appeals Court upholds California ban on affirmative action. Madeleine Albright becomes the first female Secretary of State. **MEMORABLE SONGS:** "Candle in the Wind 1997" by Elton John • "Crash into Me" by Dave Matthew Band • "How Do I Live" by Leann Rimes • "I Believe I Can Fly" by R. Kelly • "I'll Be Missing You" by Puff Daddy, Faith Evans and 112 • "Man! I Feel Like a Woman!" by Shania Twain • "MMMBop" by Hanson • "Quit Playing Games (with My Heart) by Backstreet Boys • "Tubthumping" by Chumbawamba • "Wannabe" by Spice Girls • "You Were Meant for Me" by Jewel **MEMORABLE MOVIES:** *Air Force One* • *As Good As It Gets* • *Austin Powers: International Man of Mystery* • *Good Will Hunting* • *I Know What You Did Last Summer* • *Liar Liar* • *Men in Black* • *My Best Friend's Wedding* • *Titanic* • *Tomorrow Never Dies* **SPORTS:** Super Bowl XXXI: Green Bay Packers • World Series: Florida Marlins • NBA Championship: Chicago Bulls • Stanley Cup: Detroit Red Wings • NASCAR Championship: Jeff Gordon • Wimbledon: Martina Hingis and Pete Sampras • U.S. Open: Martina Hingis and Patrick Rafter • World Figure Skating Championship: Tara Lipinski (United States) and Elvis Stojko (Canada) • PGA Championship: Davis Love III **TRANSPORTATION:** Chevrolet introduces the C5 Corvette. Boeing F-22 Raptor makes its first flight, climbing 15,000 feet in less than three minutes. **TECHNOLOGY:** Microsoft buys Hotmail. U.S. company launches first commercial spy satellite. Steve Jobs returns to Apple. **INVENTIONS:** Internet Explorer 4 web browser • AOL Instant Messenger **DISCOVERIES:** Surgeons separate Zambian Siamese twins joined at the head. Scientists clone the first primates, rhesus monkeys named Neti and Ditto. U.S. spacecraft begins exploration on Mars.

FADS: The Dancing Baby • Giga Pets and Tamagotchi virtual pets • belly shirts

---

CULTURE: A TV ratings system—TV-Y, TV-G, TV-Y7, TV-PG, TV-14, and TV-M—is introduced on cable stations and broadcast networks. Ellen DeGeneres announces she's gay. *Ally McBeal*, *Buffy the Vampire Slayer*, *King of the Hill* and *South Park* debut. Weight-loss drug Fen Phen is pulled from the market. Mike Tyson bites off Evander Holyfield's ear in a boxing match. Designer Gianni Versace is murdered.

our

1
2
3

favorites

$

MILK
$2.67/gallon

GAS
$1.29/gallon

NEW HOME
$176,200

AVERAGE INCOME
$56,902/year

MINIMUM WAGE
$5.15/hour

FAMILY
Milestones

WHERE WE LIVED: ....

....

....

JOBS WE WORKED OR YEAR IN SCHOOL: ....

....

....

CARS WE DROVE: ....

....

PEOPLE WE LOVED: ....

....

SONGS WE LOVED: ....

....

MOVIES WE LOVED: ....

....

TRIPS WE TOOK: ....

....

TECHNOLOGY WE BOUGHT: ....

....

MAJOR MILESTONES: ....

» Births: ....

....

» Graduations: ....

....

» Marriages: ....

....

» Deaths: ....

....

favorite memory...

....

....

....

....

....

19**98**

TOP NEWS STORIES: President Bill Clinton embroiled in scandal over affair with former White House intern Monica Lewinsky. Matthew Shepard, a gay Wyoming college student, is beaten to death. Bombings of U.S. Embassies in Tanzania and Kenya kill 224.

GOVERNMENT: U.S. House impeaches Clinton on perjury and obstruction of justice charges.

MEMORABLE SONGS: "All My Life" by K-Cl & Jojo • "Baby One More Time" by Britney Spears • "The Boy is Mine" by Brandy and Monica • "Gettin' Jiggy With It" by Will Smith • "Good Riddance (Time of Your Life)" by Green Day • "How's It Going to Be" by Third Eye Blind • "I Don't Want to Wait" by Paula Cole • "My Heart Will Go On" by Celine Dion • "One Week" by Barenaked Ladies • "Too Close" by Next • "Truly, Madly, Deeply" by Savage Garden • "You're Still the One" by Shania Twain **MEMORABLE MOVIES:** *Armageddon* • *The Big Lebowski* • *A Bug's Life* • *Rush Hour* • *Saving Private Ryan* • *Stepmom* • *There's Something About Mary* • *The Waterboy* • *The Wedding Singer* • *You've Got Mail* **SPORTS:** Super Bowl XXXII: Denver Broncos • NBA Championship: Chicago Bulls • Stanley Cup: Detroit Red Wings • NASCAR Championship: Jeff Gordon • World Cup: France • Wimbledon: Jana Novotná and Pete Sampras • U.S. Open: Lindsay Davenport and Patrick Rafter • World Figure Skating Championship: Michelle Kwan (United States) and Alexei Yagudin (Russia) • PGA Championship: Tiger Woods **CELEBRITY BIRTHS:** Paris Jackson • Jaden Smith **TRANSPORTATION:** Ford Motor Co. announces buyout of Volvo Cars. Workers strike at GM for seven weeks. American Airlines become the first airline to offer electronic ticketing in all countries it serves. Daimler-Benz merges with Chrysler. Toyota Camry is the top-selling car of the year. **TECHNOLOGY:** First XML programming specification is released. Microsoft releases Windows 98. Antitrust case is filed against Microsoft. Google is founded. **NEW PRODUCTS:** Game Boy Color • Sega Dreamcast • Viagra • Apple's iMac **DISCOVERIES:** The *Athena* probe finds frozen water on the moon. John Glenn returns to space. **FADS:** Furby toy • Hampster Dance website • Teletubbies **CULTURE:** J.K. Rowling's *Harry Potter and the Sorcerer's Stone* is published in the United States. *Dawson's Creek*, *Family Guy*, *Felicity*, *Sex and the City*, *That '70s Show* and *Will & Grace* debut on TV. An estimated 76 million viewers watch the last episode of *Seinfeld*.

our

1

2

3

favorites

$

MILK
$2.85/gallon

GAS
$1.12/gallon

NEW HOME
$181,900

AVERAGE INCOME
$59,589/year

MINIMUM WAGE
$5.15/hour

FAMILY Milestones

WHERE WE LIVED: ....

....

....

JOBS WE WORKED OR YEAR IN SCHOOL:

....

....

CARS WE DROVE: ....

....

PEOPLE WE LOVED: ....

....

SONGS WE LOVED: ....

....

MOVIES WE LOVED: ....

....

TRIPS WE TOOK: ....

....

TECHNOLOGY WE BOUGHT: ....

....

MAJOR MILESTONES:

» Births: ....

....

» Graduations: ....

....

» Marriages: ....

....

» Deaths: ....

....

favorite memory

....

....

....

....

1999

TOP NEWS STORIES: Eric Harris and Dylan Klebold kill 12 students and a teacher before killing themselves at Columbine High School in Littleton, Colorado. John F. Kennedy Jr. and wife Carolyn Bessette Kennedy die in a plane crash. Strongest tornado ever recorded, an F5, kills 38 in Moore, Oklahoma. **GOVERNMENT:** Administration of Panama Canal is returned to the Panamanian government. President Bill Clinton's impeachment is halted by the Senate. **MEMORABLE SONGS:** "Amazed" by Lonestar • "Believe" by Cher • "Every Morning" by Sugar Ray • "Genie in a Bottle" by Christina Aguilera • "I Want It That Way" by Backstreet Boys • "Kiss Me" by Sixpence None the Richer • "Livin' La Vida Loca" by Ricky Martin • "No Scrubs" by TLC **MEMORABLE MOVIES:** *American Beauty* • *American Pie* • *The Blair Witch Project* • *The Boondock Saints* • *Fight Club* • *The Green Mile* • *The Matrix* • *Office Space* • *Runaway Bride* • *The Sixth Sense* **SPORTS:** Super Bowl XXXIII: Denver Broncos • World Series: New York Yankees • NBA Championship: San Antonio Spurs • Stanley Cup: Dallas Stars • NASCAR Championship: Dale Jarrett • Wimbledon: Lindsay Davenport and Pete Sampras • U.S. Open: Serena Williams and Andre Agassi • World Figure Skating Championship: Maria Butyrskaya (Russia) and Alexei Yagudin (Russia) • PGA Championship: Tiger Woods **TRANSPORTATION:** Brian Jones and Bertrand Piccard make the first nonstop around-the-world hot-air balloon flight. Crossover vehicles introduced. **TECHNOLOGY:** Number of worldwide Internet users reaches 150 million. The Melissa and Chernobyl viruses infect computers. The term "blog" is coined. **NEW PRODUCTS:** MSN Messenger • Napster music sharing service • Apple's Power Mac G4 • TiVo • *Family Tree Magazine* **DISCOVERIES:** Doctors perform the first human hand transplant. *Liberty Bell 7* space capsule is discovered off the coast of Florida after 38 years.

FADS: Pokémon trading cards fly off shelves.
Reality TV phenomenon explodes in popularity.
Y2K craze spurs runs on bottled water.

CULTURE: *Law & Order: Special Victims Unit, The Sopranos, SpongeBob SquarePants, The West Wing* and *Who Wants to Be a Millionaire* debut on TV. Woodstock 1999 kicks off in Rome, NY. Opening of *Star Wars Episode I: The Phantom Menace* movie breaks box-office records, grossing $102.7 million in its first weekend. American soccer player Brandi Chastain scores game-winning penalty kick against China in women's World Cup. Lance Armstrong wins his first Tour de France.

our 1 2 3 favorites

$

MILK
$2.87/gallon

GAS
$1.22/gallon

NEW HOME
$195,800

AVERAGE INCOME
$62,636/year

MINIMUM WAGE
$5.15/hour

FAMILY Milestones

WHERE WE LIVED: ....

....

....

JOBS WE WORKED OR YEAR IN SCHOOL:

....

....

CARS WE DROVE: ....

....

PEOPLE WE LOVED: ....

....

SONGS WE LOVED: ....

....

MOVIES WE LOVED: ....

....

TRIPS WE TOOK: ....

....

TECHNOLOGY WE BOUGHT: ....

....

MAJOR MILESTONES: ....

» Births: ....

....

» Graduations: ....

....

» Marriages: ....

....

» Deaths: ....

....

favorite memory

....

....

....

....

....

20OO

TOP NEWS STORIES: Elian Gonzalez returns to Cuba with his father, ending a custody battle. *Concorde* crash kills 113 near Paris. Fears of mad cow disease result in bans on beef. **GOVERNMENT:** U.S. Supreme Court stops the Florida presidential election recount, resulting in George W. Bush winning the presidential election.

CENSUS RESULTS: U.S. population is 281,421,906. Billionth person living in India is born.

MEMORABLE SONGS: "Bent" by Matchbox 20 • "Breathe" by Faith Hill • "Everything You Want" by Vertical Horizon • "He Wasn't Man Enough" by Toni Braxton • "I Knew I Loved You" by Savage Garden • "Say My Name" by Destiny's Child • "Smooth" by Santana and Rob Thomas • "Thong Song" by Sisqó • "Who Let the Dogs Out" by Baha Men **MEMORABLE MOVIES:** *American Psycho* • *Cast Away* • *Erin Brokovich* • *How the Grinch Stole Christmas* • *Gladiator* • *Meet the Parents* • *Remember the Titans* • *Scary Movie* • *What Women Want* • *X-Men* **SPORTS:** Super Bowl XXXIV: St. Louis Rams • World Series: New York Yankees • NBA Championship: Los Angeles Lakers • Stanley Cup: New Jersey Devils • NASCAR Championship: Bobby Labonte • Wimbledon: Venus Williams and Pete Sampras • U.S. Open: Venus Williams and Marat Safin • World Figure Skating Championship: Michelle Kwan (United States) and Alexei Yagudin (Russia) • PGA Championship: Tiger Woods **CELEBRITY BIRTHS:** Noah Cyrus • Jackie Evancho • Willow Smith **TRANSPORTATION:** The last Boeing 737 rolls off the assembly line. The first hybrid car to be sold in the United States, the Honda Insight, goes on sale. **TECHNOLOGY:** America Online and Time Warner merge to form AOL Time Warner. Court case rules Microsoft violated U.S. antitrust laws by keeping "an oppressive thumb" on its competitors. Computer pioneer Datapoint files for Chapter 11 bankruptcy. ILOVEYOU virus infects computers worldwide. First resident crews enter International Space Station. **NEW PRODUCTS:** *O* magazine • The Sims • Chrysler PT Cruiser **DISCOVERIES:** Human genome deciphered and is expected to revolutionize the practice of medicine. Researchers successfully clone pigs. **FADS:** Peer-to-peer file sharing sites • Razor scooters • Geocaching **CULTURE:** *Big Brother*, *C.S.I: Crime Scene Investigation*, *Gilmore Girls*, *Malcolm in the Middle* and *Survivor* debut on TV. The final "Peanuts" comic strip is published. The NASDAQ stock market index reaches an all-time high. Madonna marries Guy Ritchie. Ellen DeGeneres and Anne Heche announce their breakup.

our

1

2

3

favorites

$

MILK
$2.78/gallon

GAS
$1.57/gallon

NEW HOME
$206,400

AVERAGE INCOME
$65,500/year

MINIMUM WAGE
$5.15/hour

FAMILY
Milestones

WHERE WE LIVED: ....

....

....

JOBS WE WORKED OR YEAR IN SCHOOL:

....

....

CARS WE DROVE:

....

PEOPLE WE LOVED:

....

SONGS WE LOVED:

....

MOVIES WE LOVED:

....

TRIPS WE TOOK: ....

....

TECHNOLOGY WE BOUGHT: ....

MAJOR MILESTONES:

» Births: ....

» Graduations: ....

» Marriages: ....

» Deaths: ....

....

favorite memory

....

....

....

....

20O1

TOP NEWS STORIES: Terrorists crash hijacked airplanes into New York City's World Trade Center and the Pentagon; a fourth hijacked plane crashes outside Pittsburgh, killing nearly 3,000. Anthrax-laced letters sent to media and government offices. Enron accounting scandal unfolds.

GOVERNMENT: George W. Bush and Dick Cheney are sworn in as president and vice president. Bush signs new tax-cut law, the largest in 20 years. USA Patriot Act becomes law. **MEMORABLE SONGS:** "All for You" by Janet Jackson • "Drops of Jupiter (Tell Me)" by Train • "Fallin'" by Alicia Keys • "Hanging by a Moment" by Lifehouse • "Hero" by Enrique Iglesias • "Jaded" by Aerosmith • "Lady Marmalade" by Christina Aguilera, Lil' Kim, Mya and Pink • "I'm Real" by Jennifer Lopez • "Thank You" by Dido **MEMORABLE MOVIES:** *A Beautiful Mind* • *Bridget Jones' Diary* • *The Fast and the Furious* • *Harry Potter and the Sorcerer's Stone* • *Legally Blonde* • *The Lord of the Rings: The Fellowship of the Ring* • *Ocean's Eleven* • *Pearl Harbor* • *The Princess Diaries* • *Shrek* **SPORTS:** Super Bowl XXXV: Baltimore Ravens • World Series: Arizona Diamondbacks • NBA Championship: Los Angeles Lakers • Stanley Cup: Colorado Avalanche • NASCAR Championship: Jeff Gordon • Wimbledon: Venus Williams and Goran Ivaniševic • U.S. Open: Venus Williams and Lleyton Hewitt • World Figure Skating Championship: Michelle Kwan (United States) and Evgeny Plushenko (Russia) • PGA Championship: David Toms **CELEBRITY BIRTHS:** Sasha Obama • Maddox Jolie-Pitt **TRANSPORTATION:** *Car and Driver* magazine creates separate "Five Best Trucks" list, topped by Ford F-Series, Chevrolet Silverado and Ford Explorer. **TECHNOLOGY:** Apple releases Mac OS X and opens its first retail stores. Wikipedia, a collaborative online encyclopedia, launches. World's first self-contained artificial heart is implanted in Robert Tools. **INVENTIONS:** Gleevec cancer drug **NEW PRODUCTS:** Simply Orange juice • *Mental Floss* magazine • Apple iPod **DISCOVERIES:** Cloning animals results in defects. National Academy of Sciences report announced global warming is on the rise. **FADS:** Bratz Dolls • Low-rise jeans • *Harry Potter* series **CULTURE:** *24*, *The Amazing Race*, and *Fear Factor* debut on TV. *The Producers* takes 12 Tony Awards. Stem-cell research is a hotly debated issue. *McCalls* magazine changes its name to *Rosie*.

our 1 2 3

favorites

MILK
$2.88/gallon

GAS
$1.38/gallon

NEW HOME
$210,000

AVERAGE INCOME
$68,300/year

MINIMUM WAGE
$5.15/hour

FAMILY
Milestones

WHERE WE LIVED: ....

....

....

JOBS WE WORKED OR YEAR IN SCHOOL: ....

....

....

CARS WE DROVE: ....

....

PEOPLE WE LOVED: ....

....

SONGS WE LOVED: ....

....

MOVIES WE LOVED: ....

....

TRIPS WE TOOK: ....

....

TECHNOLOGY WE BOUGHT: ....

....

MAJOR MILESTONES: ....

» Births: ....

....

» Graduations: ....

....

» Marriages: ....

....

» Deaths: ....

....

favorite memory...

....

....

....

....

....

20O2

TOP NEWS STORIES: U.S. and Afghan troops launch Operation Anaconda against Al-Qaeda and Taliban fighters in Afghanistan. North Korea admits to developing nuclear arms in defiance of treaty. Pennsylvania miners rescued after spending 77 hours in a dark, flooded mine shaft. Snipers kill 10 and wound others in Washington, DC area.

GOVERNMENT: President George W. Bush signs corporate reform bill in response to scandals at Enron, Arthur Anderson, Tyco, Qwest, and other corporations. Department of Homeland Security is created. No Child Left Behind Act is signed into law.

MEMORABLE SONGS: "Can't Get You Out of My Head" by Kylie Minogue • "Complicated" by Avril Lavigne • "Dilemma" by Nelly and Kelly Rowland • "Hot in Herre" by Nelly • "How You Remind Me" by Nickelback • "In the End" by Linkin Park • "Lose Yourself" by Eminem • "A Thousand Miles" by Vanessa Carlton **MEMORABLE MOVIES:** *8 Mile* • *The Bourne Identity* • *Catch Me If You Can* • *Divine Secrets of the Ya-Ya Sisterhood* • *Ice Age* • *Mr. Deeds* • *My Big Fat Greek Wedding* • *Road to Perdition* • *Spider-Man* • *Sweet Home Alabama* **SPORTS:** Super Bowl XXXVI: New England Patriots • World Series: Anaheim Angels • NBA Championship: Los Angeles Lakers • Stanley Cup: Detroit Red Wings • World Cup: Brazil • NASCAR Championship: Tony Stewart • Wimbledon: Serena Williams and Lleyton Hewitt • U.S. Open: Serena Williams and Pete Sampras • PGA Championship: Rich Beem • World Figure Skating Championships: Irina Slutskaya (Russia) and Alexei Yagudin (Russia) **CELEBRITY BIRTHS:** Prince Michael Jackson II • Romeo Beckham **TRANSPORTATION:** United Airlines, the world's second largest airline, files for bankruptcy. BMW introduces first full redesign of the Mini Cooper since its 1959 debut. **TECHNOLOGY:** U.S. health officials issue new guidelines on mammograms. Hormone replacement therapy is questioned by a study that finds increases in rates of breast cancer, heart attacks, blood clots, and strokes. **INVENTIONS:** Birth control patch • Botox **NEW PRODUCTS:** Vanilla Coke • Bluetooth earpieces for mobile phones • Roomba robot vacuum **DISCOVERIES:** 7-million-year-old human skull discovered in Chad. Hubble Space Telescope finds evidence of new type of black hole. NASA's *Mars Odyssey* space probe begins mapping Mars' surface using a thermal emission imaging system, and finds large deposit of ice. Discovery of new insect order, Mantophasmatodea, is announced. **FADS:** *American Idol TV* show launches in United States and fuels frenzy.

our
1
2
3
favorites

$

MILK
$2.88/gallon

GAS
$1.38/gallon

NEW HOME
$210,000

AVERAGE INCOME
$68,300/year

MINIMUM WAGE
$5.15/hour

FAMILY
Milestones

WHERE WE LIVED: ....

....

....

JOBS WE WORKED OR YEAR IN SCHOOL: ....

....

....

CARS WE DROVE: ....

....

PEOPLE WE LOVED: ....

....

SONGS WE LOVED: ....

....

MOVIES WE LOVED: ....

....

TRIPS WE TOOK: ....

....

TECHNOLOGY WE BOUGHT: ....

....

MAJOR MILESTONES: ....

» Births: ....

....

» Graduations: ....

....

» Marriages: ....

....

» Deaths: ....

....

favorite memory...

....

....

....

....

....

....

2003

TOP NEWS STORIES: United States invades Iraq, Baghdad falls to US troops, and Saddam Hussein is captured. Space shuttle *Columbia* explodes, killing seven astronauts. Martha Stewart is indicted for using privileged investment information and then obstructing a federal investigation. Second most widespread electrical blackout in history occurs across the Northeast and Midwest. **GOVERNMENT:** President George W. Bush signs 10-year, $350 billion tax cut package, the third largest tax cut in U.S. history. Californians oust governor Gray Davis in recall vote and elect actor Arnold Schwarzenegger to replace him. Immigration and Naturalization Service becomes U.S. Citizenship and Immigration Services. **MEMORABLE SONGS:** "Bring Me to Life" by Evanescence • "Crazy in Love" by Beyoncé and Jay-Z • "Cry Me a River" by Justin Timberlake • "Hey Ya!" by Outkast • "Ignition" by R. Kelly • "In da Club" by 50 Cent • "Miss Independent" by Kelly Clarkson • "Picture" by Kid Rock and Sheryl Crow • "Unwell" by Matchbox Twenty **MEMORABLE MOVIES:** *Bruce Almighty* • *Elf* • *Finding Nemo* • *Hulk* • *The Italian Job* • *Kill Bill* • *Love Actually* • *Old School* • *Pirates of the Caribbean* • *Seabiscuit* **SPORTS:** Super Bowl XXXVII: Tampa Bay Buccaneers • World Series: Florida Marlins • NBA Championship: San Antonio Spurs • Stanley Cup: New Jersey Devils • NASCAR Championship: Matt Kenseth • Wimbledon: Serena Williams and Roger Federer • U.S. Open: Justine Henin-Hardenne and Andy Roddick • World Figure Skating Championship: Michelle Kwan (United States) and Evgeni Plushenko (Russia) • PGA Championship: Shaun Micheel

---

TRANSPORTATION: The last Volkswagen Beetle rolls off the assembly line. Toyota introduces the Prius hybrid car to the U.S. market.

TECHNOLOGY: Apple introduces the iTunes Music Store. DVD rentals top videocassettes for the first time. MySpace launches. **INVENTIONS:** CD shredder • FluMist nasal spray vaccination **NEW PRODUCTS:** Camera phones **DISCOVERIES:** The Human Genome Project is completed, with 99 percent of the human genome sequenced to 99.99 percent accuracy. Scientists uncover the fossil of a new species of flying dinosaur in China. Three fossilized skulls discovered in Ethiopia in 1997 are identified as the oldest known human remains. The Hubble telescope detects the oldest known planet. **FADS:** Low-carb diets **CULTURE:** Recording Industry Association of America cracks down on people illegally swapping songs online. *Arrested Development*, *Cold Case*, *Extreme Makeover: Home Edition*, *Mythbusters*, *The O.C.*, *NCIS* and *Two and a Half Men* debut on TV.

our 1 2 3 favorites

$

MILK
$2.76/gallon

GAS
$1.52/gallon

NEW HOME
$243,683

AVERAGE INCOME
$59,067/year

MINIMUM WAGE
$5.15/hour

FAMILY Milestones

WHERE WE LIVED: ....

....

....

JOBS WE WORKED OR YEAR IN SCHOOL: ....

....

....

CARS WE DROVE: ....

....

PEOPLE WE LOVED: ....

....

SONGS WE LOVED: ....

....

MOVIES WE LOVED: ....

....

TRIPS WE TOOK: ....

....

TECHNOLOGY WE BOUGHT: ....

....

MAJOR MILESTONES: ....

» Births: ....

....

» Graduations: ....

....

» Marriages: ....

....

» Deaths: ....

....

favorite memory

....

....

....

....

....

....

2o**04**

TOP NEWS STORIES: U.S. troops launch attack on Falluja, a stronghold of the Iraqi insurgency. Enormous tsunami devastates Indonesia and other South Asian countries, killing more than 230,000. **GOVERNMENT:** Massachusetts becomes the first state in the country to legalize same-sex marriage. **MEMORABLE SONGS:** "Burn" by Usher • "Here Without You" by 3 Doors Down • "If I Ain't Got You" by Alicia Keys • "Let's Get it Started" by Black Eyed Peas • "The Reason" by Hoobastank • "Redneck Woman" by Gretchen Wilson • "This Love" by Maroon 5 • "The Way You Move" by Outkast • "Yeah!" by Usher, Lil Jon and Ludacris **MEMORABLE MOVIES:** *Anchorman: The Legend of Ron Burgundy* • *The Aviator* • *Fahrenheit 9/11* • *Hotel Rwanda* • *The Incredibles* • *Mean Girls* • *Million Dollar Baby* • *Napoleon Dynamite* • *National Treasure* • *The Notebook* • *The Passion of the Christ* **SPORTS:** Michael Phelps wins eight medals at the Summer Olympics in Athens. Super Bowl XXXVIII: New England Patriots • World Series: Boston Red Sox • NBA Championship: Detroit Pistons • Stanley Cup: Tampa Bay • NASCAR Championship: Kurt Busch • Wimbledon: Maria Sharapova and Roger Federer • U.S. Open: Svetlana Kuznetsova and Roger Federer • World Figure Skating Championship: Shizuka Arakawa (Japan) and Evgeni Plushenko (Russia) • PGA Championship: Vijay Singh **TRANSPORTATION:** The last Oldsmobile rolls off the assembly line. Nissan releases its first full-size truck in the United States, the Titan.

TECHNOLOGY: The social network Facebook is launched.

INVENTIONS: Oral HIV test • strapless swimming goggles **NEW PRODUCTS:** Laser levels **DISCOVERIES:** Scientists create two new elements: Ununtrium and Ununpentium. NASA announces it detected that signs of water had once covered a small crater on Mars. **FADS:** LiveStrong wristbands

CULTURE: The term "wardrobe malfunction" comes into use after Justin Timberlake ripped Janet Jackson's bodice, exposing her breast during the Super Bowl halftime show. *The Apprentice*, *The Biggest Loser*, *Desperate Housewives*, *Lost* and *Project Runway* debut on TV.

our 1 2 3 favorites

$

MILK
$3.15/gallon

GAS
$1.81/gallon

NEW HOME
$271,483

AVERAGE INCOME
$60,466/year

MINIMUM WAGE
$5.15/hour

FAMILY Milestones

WHERE WE LIVED: ....

....

....

JOBS WE WORKED OR YEAR IN SCHOOL: ....

....

....

CARS WE DROVE: ....

....

PEOPLE WE LOVED: ....

....

SONGS WE LOVED: ....

....

MOVIES WE LOVED: ....

....

TRIPS WE TOOK: ....

....

TECHNOLOGY WE BOUGHT: ....

....

MAJOR MILESTONES:

» Births: ....

....

» Graduations: ....

....

» Marriages: ....

....

» Deaths: ....

....

favorite memory

....

....

....

....

....

2oO5

TOP NEWS STORIES: Hurricane Katrina strikes Louisiana, Mississippi and Alabama, killing more than 1,800 people. Four terrorist attacks in London—three on the underground and one on a bus—kill 52 and injure more than 700. Pope John Paul II dies in April and Pope Benedict XVI (Cardinal Joseph Ratzinger) succeeds him. **GOVERNMENT:** George W. Bush is inaugurated for a second term as president after defeating Sen. John Kerry. Supreme Court Chief Justice William Rehnquist dies; John Roberts is confirmed as his successor. **MEMORABLE SONGS:** "Beverly Hills" by Weezer • "Bless the Broken Road" by Rascal Flatts • "Boulevard of Broken Dreams" by Green Day • "Don't Cha" by The Pussycat Dolls • "Gold Digger" by Kanye West • "Hollaback Girl" by Gwen Stefani • "Photograph" by Nickelback • "Since U Been Gone" by Kelly Clarkson • "You and Me" by Lifehouse • "We Belong Together" by Mariah Carey

---

MEMORABLE MOVIES: *Batman Begins* • *Brokeback Mountain* • *Chronicles of Narnia: The Lion, the Witch and the Wardrobe* • *Crash* • *King Kong* • *Madagascar* • *Walk the Line* • *Wedding Crashers*

SPORTS: Super Bowl XXXIX: New England Patriots • World Series: Chicago White Sox • NBA Championship: San Antonio Spurs • PGA Championship: Phil Mickelson • NASCAR Championship: Tony Stewart • Wimbledon: Venus Williams and Roger Federer • U.S. Open: Kim Clijisters and Roger Federer • World Figure Skating Championship: Irinia Slutskaya (Russia) and Stéphane Lambiel (Switzerland) **TRANSPORTATION:** Millionaire Steve Fossett breaks a world record by completing the fastest nonstop, non-refueled solo flight around the world in the Virgin Atlantic GlobalFlyer. **TECHNOLOGY:** YouTube launches. NASA launches the Mars Reconnaissance Orbiter. Firefox web browser gains popularity. **NEW PRODUCTS:** Google Earth • Mac Mini • Xbox 360 **DISCOVERIES:** Surgeons in France perform first human face transplant. **FADS:** Paris Hilton makes famous the phrase "That's Hot." **CULTURE:** CBS news anchor Dan Rather retires after 24 years. Cancer replaces heart disease as the No. 1 cause of death of Americans. *Bones*, *Dancing with the Stars*, *Deal or No Deal*, *Grey's Anatomy* and *How I Met Your Mother* debut on TV.

our

1

2

3

favorites

$

MILK
$3.18/gallon

GAS
$2.24/gallon

NEW HOME
$289,992

AVERAGE INCOME
$63,334/year

MINIMUM WAGE
$5.15/hour

FAMILY Milestones

WHERE WE LIVED: ....

....

....

JOBS WE WORKED OR YEAR IN SCHOOL: ....

....

....

CARS WE DROVE: ....

....

PEOPLE WE LOVED: ....

....

SONGS WE LOVED: ....

....

MOVIES WE LOVED: ....

....

TRIPS WE TOOK: ....

....

TECHNOLOGY WE BOUGHT: ....

....

MAJOR MILESTONES:

» Births: ....

....

» Graduations: ....

....

» Marriages: ....

....

» Deaths: ....

....

favorite memory...

....

....

....

....

....

20O6

TOP NEWS STORIES: Saddam Hussein executed by hanging in Iraq after being convicted of committing crimes against humanity. Twelve miners die and one survives in the Sago Mine disaster in West Virginia. **GOVERNMENT:** President George W. Bush signs a law renewing the Patriot Act. Vice President Dick Cheney accidentally shoots and wounds a lawyer during a quail hunting trip. Ben Bernanke becomes chairman of the Federal Reserve. Samuel Alito is sworn in as a Supreme Court justice. **MEMORABLE SONGS:** "Bad Day" by Daniel Powter • "Crazy" by Gnarls Barkley • "Hips Don't Lie" by Shakira • "How to Save a Life" by The Fray • "Photograph" by Nickelback • "Promiscuous" by Nelly Furtado and Timbaland • "SexyBack" by Justin Timberlake • "SOS" by Rihanna • "Unwritten" by Natasha Beddingfield • "What Hurts the Most" by Rascal Flatts • "You're Beautiful" by James Blunt **MEMORABLE MOVIES:** *Blood Diamond* • *Cars* • *Casino Royale* • *The Da Vinci Code* • *The Departed* • *The Devil Wears Prada* • *Night at the Museum* • *The Pursuit of Happyness* • *Superman Returns* **SPORTS:** Super Bowl XL: Pittsburgh Steelers • World Series: St. Louis Cardinals • NBA Championship: Miami Heat • Stanley Cup: Carolina Hurricanes • NASCAR Championship: Jimmie Johnson • World Cup: Italy • PGA Championship: Tiger Woods • Wimbledon: Amélie Mauresmo and Roger Federer • U.S. Open: Maria Sharapova and Roger Federer • Figure Skating: Kimmie Meissner (United States) and Stéphane Lambiel (Switzerland) **CELEBRITY BIRTHS:** Suri Cruise • Shiloh Jolie-Pitt • Kingston Rossdale **TRANSPORTATION:** Boeing starts major assembly of the first 787 Dreamliner airplane. Pontiac releases its first two-seat roadster, the Pontiac Solstice. GM introduces the Hummer 3.

INVENTIONS: Tesla Roadster 100, an all battery-powered sports car • infrared alcohol test • Blu-ray Discs

---

NEW PRODUCTS: Nintendo Wii • Gardasil, a cancer-preventing vaccine for human papillomavirus (HPV) • Microsoft Zune **DISCOVERIES:** *New Horizons* spacecraft is launched to study Pluto's atmosphere and surface; Pluto later loses its status as a planet. Scientists discover 375-million-year-old fish fossil that has early signs of limbs, suggesting the missing link between fish and land animals. World's tallest living tree, nearly 380 feet high, discovered in Redwood National Park. **FADS:** Sudoku • Crocs shoes **CULTURE:** Jackson Pollock's painting *No. 5, 1948* sells for a record $140 million. WB and UPN TV networks merge to form the CW. Google buys YouTube for $1.65 billion. U.S. housing prices reach their peak.

our

1

2

3

favorites

$

MILK
$3.08/gallon

GAS
$2.53/gallon

NEW HOME
$303,517

AVERAGE INCOME
$66,570/year

MINIMUM WAGE
$5.15/hour

FAMILY Milestones

WHERE WE LIVED:..

....

....

JOBS WE WORKED OR YEAR IN SCHOOL:.........

....

....

CARS WE DROVE:...

....

PEOPLE WE LOVED:..

....

SONGS WE LOVED:...

....

MOVIES WE LOVED:..

....

TRIPS WE TOOK:...

....

TECHNOLOGY WE BOUGHT:................................

....

MAJOR MILESTONES:

» Births:..

....

» Graduations:..

....

» Marriages:...

....

» Deaths:..

....

favorite memory:

....

....

....

....

....

2007

TOP NEWS STORIES: United States begins surge of 30,000 troops in Iraq to stop increasingly deadly attacks by insurgents and militias. Lewis "Scooter" Libby, former chief of staff to Vice President Dick Cheney, is found guilty of lying to FBI agents and to a grand jury in the investigation of who leaked the name of an undercover CIA agent. A student kills 32 and injures many more in the Virginia Tech massacre. **GOVERNMENT:** California Democrat Nancy Pelosi becomes the first woman Speaker of the House. Minimum wage increases for the first time in 10 years. **MEMORABLE SONGS:** "Before He Cheats" by Carrie Underwood • "Big Girls Don't Cry" by Fergie • "Buy U a Drank" by T-Pain and Yung Joc • "Girlfriend" by Avril Lavigne • "Hey There Delilah" by the Plain White T's • "Home" by Daughtry • "Irreplaceable" by Beyoncé • "The Sweet Escape" by Gwen Stefani • "Umbrella" by Rihanna (featuring Jay Z) **MEMORABLE MOVIES:** *300* • *Harry Potter and the Order of the Phoenix* • *I Am Legend* • *Juno* • *No Country for Old Men* • *Pirates of the Caribbean: At World's End* • *Ratatouille* • *Shrek the Third* • *Transformers* **SPORTS:** Super Bowl XLI: Indianapolis Colts • World Series: Boston Red Sox • NBA Championship: San Antonio Spurs • Stanley Cup: Anaheim Ducks • NASCAR Championship: Jimmie Johnson • Wimbledon: Venus Williams and Roger Federer • U.S. Open: Justine Henin and Roger Federer • PGA Championship: Tiger Woods **TRANSPORTATION:** U.S. Supreme Court rules that the EPA has authority to regulate automobile emissions. President George W. Bush signs energy bill requiring passenger vehicles sold in the United States to have fuel economy standards of 35 miles per gallon by 2020, and increasing production of ethanol and other biofuels to 36 billion gallons per year by 2022.

DISCOVERIES: Study on climate change concludes that global warming is likely caused by human activity. Scientists announce a discovery of a way to make embryonic stem cells without using embryonic stem cells.

TECHNOLOGY: NASA launches robotic spacecraft *Dawn*. HITS football helmet uses sensors and wirelessly sends data on severity and location of impacts to a PC. Microsoft releases Windows Vista. Twitter launches. **INVENTIONS:** Crop-wedding robot HortiBot • Espresso Book Machine • Kindle e-Reader **NEW PRODUCTS:** Apple iPhone • Pepsi Max • $150 XO Laptop **FADS:** Webkinz toys • Ugg boots

our

1

2

3

favorites

$

MILK
$3.50/gallon

GAS
$2.77/gallon

NEW HOME
$308,775

AVERAGE INCOME
$67,609/year

MINIMUM WAGE
$5.85/hour

FAMILY Milestones

WHERE WE LIVED: ....

....

....

JOBS WE WORKED OR YEAR IN SCHOOL: ....

....

....

CARS WE DROVE: ....

....

PEOPLE WE LOVED: ....

....

SONGS WE LOVED: ....

....

MOVIES WE LOVED: ....

....

TRIPS WE TOOK: ....

....

TECHNOLOGY WE BOUGHT: ....

....

MAJOR MILESTONES: ....

» Births: ....

....

» Graduations: ....

....

» Marriages: ....

....

» Deaths: ....

....

favorite memory...

....

....

....

....

....

20O8

TOP NEWS STORIES: Barack Obama wins the 2008 presidential election against John McCain, becoming the first African-American U.S. president. Stock markets plunge amid fears of a U.S. recession and the subprime mortgage crisis. Deadliest tornado outbreak in 23 years kills 58 in the South. Severe flooding in the Midwest causes 13 deaths and more than $6 billion in damage. Fidel Castro steps down as president of Cuba. **GOVERNMENT:** President George W. Bush signs the Emergency Economic Stabilization Act, creating a $700 billion Treasury fund to purchase failing bank assets. The Housing and Economic Recovery Act of 2008 offers mortgage assistance to subprime borrowers. California's Supreme Court rules that same-sex couples have a constitutional right to marry. **MEMORABLE SONGS:** "4 Minutes" by Madonna featuring Justin Timberlake • "Apologize" by OneRepublic • "Bleeding Love" by Leona Lewis • "Bubbly" by Colbie Caillat • "Burnin' Up" by the Jonas Brothers • "I Kissed a Girl" by Katy Perry • "Love Song" by Sara Bareilles • "Low" by Flo Rida and T-Pain • "No One" by Alicia Keys • "Viva la Vida" by Coldplay **MEMORABLE MOVIES:** *The Curious Case of Benjamin Button* • *The Dark Knight* • *Hancock* • *Indiana Jones and the Kingdom of the Crystal Skull* • *Iron Man* • *Kung Fu Panda* • *Mamma Mia!* • *Sex and the City* • *Slumdog Millionaire* • *Twilight* • *WALL-E* **SPORTS:** Super Bowl XLII: New York Giants • World Series: Philadelphia Phillies • NBA Championship: Boston Celtics • World Figure Skating Championship: Mao Asada (Japan) and Jeffrey Buttle (Canada) • Stanley Cup: Detroit Red Wings • Wimbledon: Venus Williams and Rafael Nadal • U.S. Open: Serena Williams and Roger Federer • NASCAR Championship: Jimmie Johnson • PGA Championship: Pádraig Harrington **TRANSPORTATION:** Price of oil hits $100 per barrel for first time. Delta Air Lines merges with Northwest Airlines, forming the world's largest commercial carrier. **TECHNOLOGY:** Bill Gates steps down from daily duties at Microsoft to concentrate on philanthropy. Apple's App Store opens. Android smartphones hit the market. **INVENTIONS:** Tesla Motors releases its all-electric Roadster car. Company in Denmark develops a way to turn pig urine into plastic. **NEW PRODUCTS:** Flip video camera • MacBook Air • personalized M&Ms **DISCOVERIES:** Large Hadron Collider, the world's largest particle accelerator, runs for the first time. NASA discovers a remnant of the most recent supernova, from about 140 years ago.

FADS: Neon-colored clothing and makeup •
Vampires, popularized by the *Twilight* series
• Barack Obama's Hope poster by Shepard Fairey

our

1

2

3

favorites

$

MILK
$3.79/gallon

GAS
$3.21/gallon

NEW HOME
$288,917

AVERAGE INCOME
$68,424/year

MINIMUM WAGE
$6.55/hour

FAMILY
Milestones

WHERE WE LIVED: ....

....

....

JOBS WE WORKED OR YEAR IN SCHOOL: ....

....

....

CARS WE DROVE: ....

....

PEOPLE WE LOVED: ....

....

SONGS WE LOVED: ....

....

MOVIES WE LOVED: ....

....

TRIPS WE TOOK: ....

....

TECHNOLOGY WE BOUGHT: ....

....

MAJOR MILESTONES:

» Births: ....

....

» Graduations: ....

....

» Marriages: ....

....

» Deaths: ....

....

favorite memory

....

....

....

....

20O9

TOP NEWS STORIES: H1N1 (aka Swine flu) pandemic emerges. Unemployment at a 16-year high. U.S. Army psychiatrist Maj. Nidal Malik Hasan goes on a shooting spree at Fort Hood Army base in Texas, killing 13 and injuring 29. Michael Jackson dies at age 50. After striking a flock of geese, US Airways Flight 1549 is forced to land in the Hudson river and the pilot, Chesley B. "Sully" Sullenberger, is hailed as a hero.

GOVERNMENT: Barack Obama and Joe Biden inaugurated as president and vice president. U.S. Senate approves the nomination of Sonia Sotomayor to the Supreme Court, making her the first Latino and third woman appointed to the court. Iowa, New Hampshire and Vermont legalize same-sex marriage. **MEMORABLE SONGS:** "Boom Boom Pow" and "I Gotta Feeling" by The Black Eyed Peas • "Haven't Met You Yet" by Michael Bublé • "I Dreamed a Dream" by Susan Boyle • "I'm Yours" by Jason Mraz • "Just Dance" and "Poker Face" by Lady Gaga • "Love Story" and "You Belong With Me" by Taylor Swift • "Single Ladies" by Beyoncé • "Use Somebody" by Kings of Leon • "You Found Me" by The Fray **MEMORABLE MOVIES:** *2012* • *Avatar* • *Ice Age: Dawn of the Dinosaurs* • *The Hangover* • *Harry Potter and the Half-Blood Prince* • *New Moon* • *Sherlock Holmes* • *Up* **SPORTS:** Super Bowl XLIII: Pittsburgh Steelers • World Series: New York Yankees • NBA Championship: Los Angeles Lakers • Stanley Cup: Pittsburgh Penguins • NASCAR Championship: Jimmie Johnson • Wimbledon: Serena Williams and Roger Federer • U.S. Open: Kim Clijsters and Juan Martín del Potro • PGA Championship: Y.E. Yang **TRANSPORTATION:** General Motors files for bankruptcy and announces closure of 14 U.S. plants. **TECHNOLOGY:** Microsoft releases Windows 7. Farmville and Mafia Wars Facebook apps are created. *Avatar* popularizes digital 3-D movies. Two billion iPhone apps are downloaded. **INVENTIONS:** Scientists create a vaccine that seems to reduce the risk of contracting AIDS. **NEW PRODUCTS:** McDonald's McCafe coffee • Scotch Fur Fighter **DISCOVERIES:** Scientists find water on the moon during NASA's LCROSS mission. A special court rules that vaccinations do not cause autism. **FADS:** flavored waters • Kardashians • leggings **CULTURE:** Analog TV broadcasts in the United States end. *Castle*, *Glee*, *The Jersey Shore* and *Modern Family* debut. Soap opera *Guiding Light* ends after 57 years on TV.

our 1 2 3 favorites

$

MILK
$3.19/gallon

GAS
$2.32/gallon

NEW HOME
$268,233

AVERAGE INCOME
$67,967/year

MINIMUM WAGE
$7.25/hour

FAMILY
Milestones

WHERE WE LIVED: ....

....

....

JOBS WE WORKED OR YEAR IN SCHOOL: ....

....

....

CARS WE DROVE: ....

....

PEOPLE WE LOVED: ....

....

SONGS WE LOVED: ....

....

MOVIES WE LOVED: ....

....

TRIPS WE TOOK: ....

....

TECHNOLOGY WE BOUGHT: ....

....

MAJOR MILESTONES:

» Births: ....

....

» Graduations: ....

....

» Marriages: ....

....

» Deaths: ....

....

favorite memory...

....

....

....

....

....

2o10

TOP NEWS STORIES: 7.0 magnitude Earthquake devastates Haiti, killing more than 230,000 people. The Deepwater Horizon oil platform explodes in the Gulf of Mexico, resulting in the largest oil spill in history. WikiLeaks publishes covert and classified material online. 33 miners trapped underground in Chile mining accident are brought back to the surface after a record 69 days. **GOVERNMENT:** Health care reform bill passes.

CENSUS RESULTS: U.S. population reaches 308,745,538.

MEMORABLE SONGS: "Airplanes" by B.o.B. • "Bad Romance" by Lady Gaga • "California Gurls" and "Teenage Dream" by Katy Perry • "Empire State of Mind" by Jay-Z featuring Alicia Keys • "Hey, Soul Sister" by Train • "Just the Way You Are" by Bruno Mars • "Love the Way You Lie" by Eminem featuring Rihanna • "Mine" by Taylor Swift • "Need You Now" by Lady Antebellum • "OMG" by Usher • "Tik Tok" by Kesha

MEMORABLE MOVIES: *Alice in Wonderland • Harry Potter and the Deathly Hallows: Part 1 • Inception • Iron Man 2 • Shrek Forever After • Toy Story 3*

SPORTS: Super Bowl XLIV: New Orleans Saints • World Series: San Francisco Giants • NBA Championship: Los Angeles Lakers • Stanley Cup: Chicago Blackhawks • World Cup: Spain • NASCAR Championship: Jimmie Johnson • Wimbledon: Serena Williams and Rafael Nadal • U.S. Open: Kim Clijsters and Rafael Nadal • PGA Championship: Martin Kaymer **TRANSPORTATION:** Solar Impulse completes the first 24-hour flight by a solar-powered plane. Chevrolet Volt electric car goes on sale. **TECHNOLOGY:** Microsoft releases the Kinect, a controller-free video game system. 3-D TVs introduced. **INVENTIONS:** Square, a tiny magnetic credit-card reader that attaches to a smartphone • Google's driverless car • first synthetic cell **FADS:** Justin Bieber • Silly Bandz

NEW PRODUCTS: Tablet computers, including Apple's iPad • computer engineer Barbie

our 1 2 3 favorites

$

MILK
$3.25/gallon

GAS
$2.74/gallon

NEW HOME
$271,517

AVERAGE INCOME
$/year

MINIMUM WAGE
$7.25/hour

FAMILY
Milestones

WHERE WE LIVED: ....

....

....

JOBS WE WORKED OR YEAR IN SCHOOL: ....

....

....

CARS WE DROVE: ....

....

PEOPLE WE LOVED: ....

....

SONGS WE LOVED: ....

....

MOVIES WE LOVED: ....

....

TRIPS WE TOOK: ....

....

TECHNOLOGY WE BOUGHT: ....

....

MAJOR MILESTONES: ....

» Births: ....

....

» Graduations: ....

....

» Marriages: ....

....

» Deaths: ....

....

favorite memory

....

....

....

....

2011

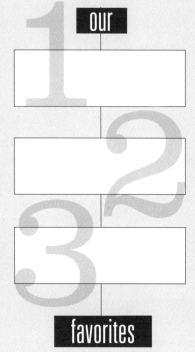

our

1

2

3

favorites

$

MILK
$__.___/gallon

GAS
$__.___/gallon

NEW HOME
$_____,_____

AVERAGE INCOME
$___,_____/year

MINIMUM WAGE
$__.___/hour

REMEMBER THAT?

FAMILY
Milestones

WHERE WE LIVED: ....

....

....

JOBS WE WORKED OR YEAR IN SCHOOL: ....

....

....

CARS WE DROVE: ....

....

PEOPLE WE LOVED: ....

....

SONGS WE LOVED: ....

....

MOVIES WE LOVED: ....

....

TRIPS WE TOOK: ....

....

TECHNOLOGY WE BOUGHT: ....

....

MAJOR MILESTONES: ....

» Births: ....

....

» Graduations: ....

....

» Marriages: ....

....

» Deaths: ....

....

favorite memory.

....

....

....

....

....

2o12

_____
_____
_____
_____
_____
_____
_____
_____
_____
_____
_____
_____
_____
_____
_____
_____
_____
_____
_____
_____
_____
_____
_____
_____
_____
_____
_____
_____
_____

our

1
2
3

favorites

$

MILK
$__.___/gallon

GAS
$__.___/gallon

NEW HOME
$_____,_____

AVERAGE INCOME
$___,_____/year

MINIMUM WAGE
$__.___/hour

FAMILY Milestones

WHERE WE LIVED: ....

....

....

JOBS WE WORKED OR YEAR IN SCHOOL:

....

....

CARS WE DROVE: ....

....

PEOPLE WE LOVED: ....

....

SONGS WE LOVED: ....

....

MOVIES WE LOVED: ....

....

TRIPS WE TOOK: ....

....

TECHNOLOGY WE BOUGHT: ....

....

MAJOR MILESTONES: ....

» Births: ....

....

» Graduations: ....

....

» Marriages: ....

....

» Deaths: ....

....

favorite memory...

....

....

....

....

20**13**

our

1

2

3

favorites

 $

MILK
$__.___/gallon

GAS
$__.___/gallon

NEW HOME
$_____,_____

AVERAGE INCOME
$___,_____/year

MINIMUM WAGE
$__.___/hour